When We Need Pictures of Jesus

A Study of Art, Worship &
the Second Commandment

Jeffrey J. Meyers

When We Need Pictures of Jesus
A Study of Art, Worship and
the Second Commandment
By Jeffrey J. Meyers

Copyright © 2024 Jeffrey J. Meyers
Athanasius Press
715 Cypress Street
West Monroe, Louisiana, 71291
www.athanasiuspress.org

Cover design and typesetting: Rachel Rosales

ISBN: 978-1-957726-16-8

Scripture quotations are from The ESV® Bible (The Holy Bible, English Standard Version®), copyright © 2001 by Crossway, a publishing ministry of Good News Publishers. Used by permission. All rights reserved.

Printed in the United States of America.

Quick Reference

Introduction

I never read a book before reviewing it — it prejudices a man so. —Sydney Smith

In this little book I seek to accomplish two objectives. I will present a case in favor of a restricted use of images of Jesus in art and education. That will mean answering common objections in Reformed circles against all use of pictures of Jesus. Those popular arguments are found in Peter Barnes's pamphlet, *Seeing Jesus: The Case Against Pictures of Our Lord Jesus Christ.*[1] My pur-

---

1. Peter Barnes, *Seeing Jesus: The Case Against Pictures of Our Lord Jesus Christ* (Edinburgh: Banner of Truth Trust, 1990). Even though this booklet is currently out of print, the arguments presented by Barnes are commonly used in Reformed circles to prohibit all pictures of Jesus. There are a few idiosyncratic arguments in *Seeing Jesus.* But even those are worth examining because they mirror the kinds of opinions often expressed in this debate.

pose is to demonstrate that the arguments he marshals in support of his thesis—that all pictures of Jesus, *regardless of their intended use*, necessarily involve a violation of the second commandment—are unsound and extra-biblical. Intertwined with my critique of Barnes I offer biblical and theological arguments in support of the *limited* use of pictures of Jesus for the purposes of art and education. I believe that a controlled use of representations of Jesus can be vindicated biblically and theologically.

I will defend the position that representations of the historical Christ, especially when depicted in a *Bible-revealed historical setting*, are not violations of the second commandment and may be utilized for educational and artistic purposes. Pictures like we find in many children's Sunday school curricula and story Bibles do not lead to or encourage idolatry in our children. Artistic depictions of the mighty acts of God such as we find in Rembrandt and others are not graven images that people bow down to or serve, nor are they attempts to capture the divinity of Jesus on canvas. For example, when we see the biblical-historical fact of Christ's baptism as it is artistically depicted in a stained-glass window at church, this aids our *memory* and helps us to *recall* this incident in the life of Jesus. No idolatry is necessarily involved.

These kinds of artistic and illustrative representations of Christ are a far cry from Eastern Orthodox iconography, which attempts to *mediate* the divine presence through portrait-like images, and which encourage men and women to worship God through such mediating icons. Similarly, Roman Catholic images are intended to be links between heaven and earth and it is in that capacity that they are venerated. A similar error occurs in American Evangelical religion wherever "portraits" of Jesus are common. "Portraits" such as Sallmon's that we find in so many popular Evangelical contexts invite abuse. Jesus' face dominates the picture—a blond-haired, blue-eyed Jesus with an aura of light surrounding his head stares dreamily off into the distance. Such "portraits" are devoid of any historical context. They are often used as aids to private devotion, and as such are indeed violations of the second commandment. Anytime an image or picture of anything or anyone is used as a *medium* through which to *communicate with* or *worship* God, such an image becomes a graven image and falls under the prohibition of the second commandment.

I am convinced that the views I have just summarized are biblical and consistent with Reformed theology. But there are those who disagree on both counts. Herein lies the necessity for my analysis. Peter Barnes and others believe that all pictures of Jesus are unbiblical and out of accord with Reformed tradition. I will answer Barnes's biblical arguments shortly.

Mea Culpa

I am a Reformed Pastor of a Presbyterian church. I am committed to what is commonly called the "regulative principle of worship" as it is summarized in the Westminster Confession of Faith, Chapter 21, Article 1-3, and the Westminster Larger Catechism, Questions 108 and 109.[2] Many years ago I taught and defended the no-pictures-of-Jesus position that Barnes does in his pamphlet. At that time, I considered such a viewpoint as part and parcel with Reformed theology and practice. I even led a "mini crusade" against all pictures of Jesus in the Sunday School curriculum of the presbyterian church I attended. The reason I mention this is to un-

---

2. The regulative principle of worship is often formulated more narrowly than warranted by the precise wording of the Westminster Standards. See James B. Jordan's three books on this subject: *Liturgical Nestorianism: A Critical Review of* Worship in the Presence of God (Niceville, FL: Transfiguration Press, 1994), *The Liturgy Trap: The Bible Versus Mere Tradition In Worship* (Monroe, LA: Athanasius Press, 2008), and *Theses on Worship: Notes Toward the Reformation of Worship* (Niceville, FL: Transfiguration Press, 1994).

derscore that I understand that those who defend such a view have a great deal of emotional investment tied up in this issue. Adherence to the no-pictures-of-Jesus-under-any-circumstances-or-for-any-purpose point of view was for me proof that I was truly Reformed.

Today, however, I am compelled by the Scriptures and the best of our Reformed heritage to confess that I was mistaken. It's not easy to admit our mistakes. I have left a string of friends behind in past churches that I convinced at one time or another that all pictures of Jesus were idolatry. Now I have to swallow my pride and confess my error. This is not unusual. Christians ought to grow and mature in their understanding of the faith, which means that they may have to confess that many of their earlier views were wrong and retract them. Augustine once wrote:

> Cicero, the prince of Roman orators says of someone that "He never uttered a word which he would wish to recall." High Praise indeed!—but more applicable to a complete ass than to a genuinely wise man.... If God permit me, I shall gather together and point out, in a work specially devoted to this purpose, all the things that justly displease me in my books: then men will see that I am far from being a biased judge in my own case.... For I am the sort of man who writes

because he has made progress, and who makes progress—by writing (*Epistle* 143.2-3).[3]

Augustine did just what he had proposed. At age 75 he wrote his famous *Retractions* in which he acknowledged the progress he had made in his understanding of the Christian faith and corrected the errors that necessarily clutter the path of one who is constantly learning. Augustine's honesty ought to be an example to all Christians, especially elders and pastors.

I'm More Reformed Than You Are!

Before I begin with my critique of Barnes, I have a few preliminary observations to make. First, I would like to register some strong reservations about the idea that those who hold the radical no-pictures-of-Jesus position are the most consistently Reformed. To insist that Reformed churches that forbid images of Jesus for any and all purposes are more genuinely Reformed than others, or to argue that they alone are remaining true to the regulative principle of worship, draws the boundaries of Reformed orthodoxy too tightly. Such

____

3. Quoted in Peter Brown, *Augustine of Hippo* (Berkeley, CA: University of California Press, 1967), p. 353.

a narrow viewpoint is historically untenable.[4] To measure the faithfulness of a church or individual to the Reformed "regulative principle of worship" by determining whether pictures of the humanity of Jesus are being used in the Sunday School will not stand the test

---

4. Has the historic Reformed church really rejected all artistic and illustrative pictures of Jesus? If it has, where are published theological and biblical apologies for this viewpoint? Why don't we have such a train of published works stretching back to the Reformation? Why didn't the Reformed churches condemn men like Rembrandt for their artistic representations of Jesus? If making pictorial representations of Jesus for educational and artistic purposes constitutes the heinous sin of *idolatry*, we ought to expect some very well-thought-out Reformed critiques of such a violation of the second commandment. I have asked prominent Reformed men for examples of such works, and I have searched the literature with minimal success. Virtually all the historic Reformed literature relating to this subject concerns the use of pictures of Jesus as aids to public and private worship. Note that Barnes does not cite one single book or essay *devoted to* the defense of this radical viewpoint. In fact, as I hope to show in this essay, only one of his citations can be considered an unambiguous attack on pictures of Jesus in non-devotional, non-liturgical contexts—Amy Carmichael's comments. This means, of course, that the essay by Barnes is one of the very few published defenses of the no-pictures-of-Jesus doctrine available to modern Christians. All the more reason why it should be rigorously examined.

of the best of Reformed tradition. Yet this issue has in fact been used as a litmus test by many Reformed Baptists and Presbyterians.

Interestingly enough, one of the most rigorous twentieth-century expositions of the regulative principle of worship, *The Biblical Doctrine of Worship* (published by the Reformed Presbyterian Church in North America [RPCNA] in 1974), not only does not contain any condemnation of non-liturgical, non-devotional pictures of Jesus, but actually questions whether the Larger Catechism, Question 109, really forbids *all* physical and mental images of the humanity of Christ.[5] Presumably, among the eminent Covenanter theologians of the RPCNA, having pictures of Jesus in Sunday School literature was not considered the blasphemous act of idolatry that some today would like us to think it is. Their symposium assails idolatry on virtually every page but mentions pictures of the humanity of Jesus only in passing, and then only to raise doubts about the propriety of extending the Westminster standards to cover such artistic and educational images.

---

5. Donald Weilersbacher, "Implication of Exodus 20:3-6 for the Doctrine of Worship," in *The Biblical Doctrine of Worship* (Reformed Presbyterian Church of North America: Committee on Worship, 1974), 22.

I will return to the RPCNA symposium a little later. I simply wish to illustrate that even among the "truly" Reformed Presbyterians (I trust no one will mistake the Psalm-singing Covenanters of the RPCNA as nominally Reformed!) there is some honest hesitation on this issue. My point: the genuinely Reformed view should not be erroneously and irresponsibly identified with the radical no-pictures-of-Jesus viewpoint. It's not that simple. The historical evidence is not so clear-cut, as I hope to show near the end of this booklet.

Idols are for Destruction

My second preliminary observation is that the controversy over pictures of Jesus obviously has some significant *practical* implications. If all representations of Jesus, no matter what their intended purpose, are violations of the second commandment, then it necessarily follows that to create, possess, or use such representations constitutes the heinous sin of idolatry. I'm not sure if our brethren who hold such a view have considered the implications. If the presence of pictures of Jesus in a Sunday school curriculum is a violation of the second commandment, then it is *idolatry*. It is not merely an unbiblical practice, nor simply a harmful custom (like "altar calls") with which we disagree. It is idolatry. And churches that have stained glass windows with pictures of Jesus are involved in *idolatrous* practices.

Idolatry calls for radical measures. Churches understanding the implications of such a position must remove all pictures of Jesus from the physical environment of the church. Sunday School curricula which utilize pictures of Jesus as illustrative aids are trafficking in idolatry and may not be used or supported. Flannel-graph pictures of Jesus must go. Any Christian literature that a church might desire to utilize, which nevertheless may contain an occasional picture of Jesus must be corrected: the faces of every picture of Jesus must be rubbed out or blackened.[6] Children's Bibles that contain illustrations of Jesus ought to be forbidden or else the pages with the idolatrous representations must be torn out. The same holds true with the popular illustrated children's story Bibles. Children and adults must be taught how to react to pictures of Jesus that they may inadvertently come across: quickly put your hand over the face of Jesus so as not to be polluted by idolatry or tear out the page in the spirit of

---

6. This is a typical solution for those who reject all pictures of Jesus. I have always wondered, however, why blacken only the faces of these images? Is there something especially dangerous about depicting Jesus with a face?

the iconoclastic crusaders of the radical Reformation. Some of these very practices are common among those who believe that all pictures of Jesus are idolatrous.

If, on the other hand, non-liturgical pictures of Jesus are not contrary to God's law, then all the aforementioned measures constitute one massive *legalistic* burden on the Christian community—legalistic in the sense that they go *beyond* God's Word by demanding obedience to man-made rules: "touch not; taste not; handle not; look not." Not only are they a legalistic burden, but the complete absence of pictures of Jesus may have some unfortunate theological implications for the training of our children. The comprehensive absence of any representations of the humanity of Jesus in a curriculum of ecclesiastical education will surely influence the theological development of children and adults (*lex orandi, lex credendi*) toward docetism.[7] A

---

7. The Latin tag *lex orandi, lex credendi* literally means "the law of prayer, the law of belief." The idea is that the practices that a community consistently follows (its *lex orandi*) will eventually influence what it believes and confesses (its *lex credendi*). If children are consistently denied representations that remind them that Jesus was (and is) a real human being (all the while seeing pictures of real disciples), then the possibility at least exists for them to develop views of Christ at odds with the classical orthodox belief that He assumed a genuine, depictable, cre-

docetic view of the person of Christ is one that disparages the physical, material, space-time reality of his humanity. As I will argue below, how can anyone who is constantly denied representations of the human Jesus—when representations of every other historical biblical character fill the pages of his Sunday school material—how can anyone, I ask, avoid the tendency to develop docetic views of the nature of Christ? Wouldn't children wonder? Why do I see pictures of Peter and the other disciples, but not Jesus? Why is he always off the page? Was he a real man? Why is his face always blackened out? Did he look like other men or was he something strange and weird?

Prejudicing the Case

In Barnes's introductory paragraph, one which bears the subtitle "Seeing Jesus," he cites John 12:20-21, where some Greeks asked to "see Jesus." Barnes explains that Jesus denied their request to *see* him and instead *preached* to them.

> In the last week before the crucifixion, some Greeks came to Jerusalem to celebrate Passover.

---

ated human nature. Not that it *must* lead to such a confession. But the potential is there.

They met with Philip, one of the twelve apostles, and asked him, "Sir, we wish to see Jesus" (John 12:20-21). Jesus responded not by granting them a closer look at his physical appearance, but by giving a discourse on the meaning of his death, and the need to die in order to live (see John 12:23ff). Today the request of the Greek inquirers has taken on a more literal and less desirable meaning, and the response of the Church has departed from that given by her Lord. Even in churches which trace their spiritual heritage back to the Reformation there has been a widespread acceptance of pictorial representations of Christ.[8]

If by referencing this text Barnes wishes to suggest that it has some bearing on the question of pictures of Jesus, his irresponsible handling of the Word of God must be exposed as a subterfuge. The idea that these Greeks desired something idolatrous is ludicrous. But this is exactly what Barnes explicitly suggests. He necessarily implies that these men desired to *get a prohibited look at* Jesus. Surely, the *normal* meaning of their request, "We wish to see Jesus," is too obvious for extended comment: these men desired to meet and talk

---

8. Barnes, *Seeing Jesus*, 1.

with Jesus. The *text* contains nothing whatsoever that would even remotely suggest that Jesus was rebuking them for wanting to gaze illicitly at his physical constitution!

Why then does Barnes mention this biblical story? My first inclination was to give him the benefit of the doubt. I thought that he was merely using it as an illustration, an illustrative foil to draw the reader into his topic. But if that's true, why does he *interpret* it as an admonition to the Greeks not to seek a physical peek? Why does Barnes explain the *meaning* of the story so as to suggest that Jesus rebuked them for wanting to *look* at him?

In the next sentence Barnes goes on to claim that by making pictorial representations of Christ, "the response of the church has departed *from that given by her Lord*"[9]—as if to suggest that Jesus' comments in John 12:20-21 were directed toward the question of whether it is appropriate to artistically depict his humanity! Here again, if we take Barnes's words at face value, he is claiming that in John 12, Jesus makes a definitive statement about the sinful desire to look at his outward appearance (and, by implication, about pictures of himself). How utterly absurd this kind of in-

---

9. Barnes, 1, emphasis mine.

terpretation is anyone can see for himself by checking any reputable commentary on this passage! To suggest that Jesus rebuked these Greeks because they wanted to *look* at him is downright silly.

What if I were to argue *for* pictures of Jesus by presenting as evidence another passage from the same Gospel? Consider the following hypothetical argument and note how closely it parallels Barnes's introductory paragraph:

> In response to Nathaniel's sarcastic comment about the possibility of anything good coming out of Nazareth, Philip said to him, "Come and *see*" (John 1:46). Here Philip responds to Nathaniel's skepticism by urging him *to look at* Jesus' physical appearance. Thus, we see how important it is that people who desire to come to Christ be able to see a picture of Jesus. Today, too many Christians fail to follow the example of Philip in leading people to Christ. They have departed from the godly response of Philip refusing to allow people to see pictures of Jesus.

How is my hypothetical argument using John 1:46 essentially different from Barnes's use of John 12:20-21? Right off the bat, then, Barnes seriously confuses the issue, (mis)using the very Word of God by carelessly suggesting an impossible interpretation (or application) of John 12:20-21. Unfortunately, this kind of prejudicing of the case by misinterpreting Holy Scripture will likely influence the simple Christian reader who seldom feels constrained to question an author who quotes the Bible to back up his assertions.

Much more could be said by way of introduction; but one last comment is in order. If you want to get the most out of my critique, I suggest that you have a copy of Barnes nearby in order to check the accuracy of my comments.

The Second Commandment: A Clear Principle?

Who can imagine that the Scriptures still carry any weight when one is obligated to assent to teachers who concoct arguments without reference to the Scriptures?
—Martin Luther

Barnes rightly rejects any rationale for pictures of Jesus based on expediency or supposed usefulness. I wholeheartedly concur. He seeks to isolate "a relevant biblical principle that excludes any justification for consideration based upon expediency."[1] Where shall we find such a biblical principle? He suggests that the second commandment provides us with such a "clear principle" from which to decide the issue. He then quotes the second commandment.

-----

1. Barnes, 1.

"You shall not make for yourself any carved image, or any likeness of anything that is in heaven above, or that is in the earth beneath, or that is in the water under the earth; you shall not bow down to them nor serve them. For I, Yahweh your God, am a jealous God, visiting the iniquity of the fathers on the children to the third and fourth generations of those who hate Me, but showing mercy to thousands, to those who love Me and keep My commandments (Exod. 20:4-6; see Deut. 5:8-10).[2]

Now, I agree that the *interpretation* of the second commandment is crucial to the controversy. But that's just the point of the debate—the *interpretation* of the commandment. To suggest that merely *quoting* the commandment provides a "clear principle" that *automatically* decides the outcome of the controversy is a bit naive. After all, the commandment does not say, "Thou shalt not make pictures of Jesus." Note well, please, that it doesn't even say, "Thou shalt not make pictures of God." There's more to it than that. The commandment must be *interpreted*.

If the question were whether we could *worship* God *through the medium of visual representations*, then

---

2. Barnes, 2.

the issue would be clear-cut. The phrase "you shall not bow down to them nor serve them" clearly qualifies the first part of the commandment which forbids the fashioning of images. Images may not be fashioned and utilized for a specific purpose—Yahweh may not be served or worshiped by means of graven images.

Images of Things in Heaven and Earth

After all, it is clear that the Israelites did, in fact, fashion carved and molten images in *the likeness of things in heaven*. To name just two examples: Cherubim were carved on the golden interior walls of the Holy Place in the Temple (1 Kings 6:29), and the faces of the cherubim decorated the "water chariots" outside in the courtyard (1 Kings 7:28ff.). They also made *images of things on earth*. Consider these obvious examples: pomegranate trees on the walls of the tabernacle and temple (1 Kings 6:29), twelve oxen holding up the brazen sea (1 Kings 7:23-25), a lampstand with bowls carved to look like almond blossoms (Exod. 25:33, 34; 37:19, 20), and lily blossoms crowning the two capitals at the entrance of the Temple (1 Kings 7:22). If that were not enough, all of these carved images (1 Kings 6:29) decorated the environment of worship! If the presence of these carved images in the environment of the tabernacle and temple was not a violation of the second commandment ("you shall not make for your-self any carved image"), then this first part of the commandment cannot be made into an absolute prohibition of all carved images without reference to their use!

The commandment, then, very clearly mandates that God should not be *worshiped or served* through any carved image—any humanly fashioned, artistic medium. (No doubt the background to this commandment is the pagan practice of constructing idols to visualize or conjure up the gods to the worshipper.) Consequently, if the present controversy regarding pictures of Jesus were over *worshiping* Jesus through visual representations, then a simple appeal to the second commandment would suffice. The second commandment forbids "bowing down to" and "serving" humanly crafted images. The second commandment, therefore, clearly forbids "bowing down to" and "serving" artistic representations of Jesus. This effectively rules out all *liturgical* and *devotional* uses of pictures and "portraits" of Jesus. But it does *not*, contrary to Barnes, *clearly* rule out all pictures of Jesus that are not used in private or public worship. This point is crucial.

No orthodox *Reformed* theologian or pastor that I know advocates the *liturgical* use of pictures of Jesus as aids in public worship or the *devotional* use of them in private worship. I had a roommate in college who had a picture of Jesus that he used for personal devotions. Actually, it was more like a "portrait." When he got up in the morning he would pray to Jesus *through* the picture. As he described it to me, if the picture appeared to be smiling, he knew that Jesus was pleased with his prayer. But if my roommate felt like the picture of Jesus was frowning, then he interpreted this as evidence of God's displeasure. Here we have a clear example of the devotional abuse of an image of Christ. The man was using this image as a medium through which to discover God's will, to conjure him up, so to speak. This would be a clear example of a violation of the second commandment. (I believe that most "portraits" of Jesus invite abuse and ought to be avoided. More on that later.)

Most Reformed theologians believe that this commandment implies the prohibition of the presence of representations of Jesus anywhere in the environment of worship, public and private. They have argued in the past that if pictures of Jesus decorated the environment of corporate worship, even if those who lead the worship service do not intend to use the pictures as *media* through which Jesus is worshiped, nevertheless, the danger exists that weaker Christians within the congregation may be tempted to worship the Lord through the medium of the images that are present. This makes good sense. The example of the Old Testament temple and tabernacle, however, filled with images by God's command, causes me to question the strictness of such precautions. Should all images whatsoever be banished from the environment of worship? Didn't Yahweh know that the Israelites would be tempted to idolatry with all those images of things in heaven and things on earth adorning the tabernacle and temple from the courtyard to the Holy of Holies? Surely the hard-hearted Old Covenant Israelites would be more susceptible to temptation by such images than New Covenant believers.

Clarifying the Precise Issue

The current controversy, however, has to do with using pictures of Jesus in didactic and artistic settings, not liturgical settings. The pertinent questions are: May we portray Christ in art? May we represent him in educational visual aids? Approached with these questions in mind, the second commandment is not as "clear" as Barnes implies. At least a *prima facie* reading of the second commandment does not unambiguously forbid artistic and educational uses of pictures of God. In fact, if anyone wants to insist that the second commandment clearly forbids every kind of image of God whatsoever, no matter how it may be used, then one must logically deduce from the precise language of the second commandment that *all pictures* of anything whatsoever "in heaven, on earth, or under the earth" are prohibited, regardless of their intended use.

In other words, if one does not restrict the meaning of the second commandment regarding the intended use of the range of images mentioned, then *all* pictures of anything whatsoever will be idolatrous, including blueprints of houses, all photographs, and your child's stick-figure doodles as well. There's no getting around it. The commandment does not restrict the prohibition against images to representations of God! The commandment prohibits all representations of anything whatsoever. But once you understand that the second commandment intends to debar anyone from *worshiping* God by means of any image created by man, then the question of the legitimacy of other uses for representations must be determined from *other* Scriptural passages and principles.

Furthermore, when Barnes warns that "the whole Bible thunders out the same message. . . the true God is not to be worshiped by means of images" and references a long string of passages, he is firing into the dirt (at least with respect to most Reformed churches). Barnes could catalog a series of Bible passages ten pages long that forbade *worshiping* God through images and yet he would be no closer to answering the question of whether representations of Christ could be used for *other* purposes!

Unfortunately, Barnes never really makes any substantial distinction between the three uses for pictures of Jesus: 1) their *liturgical* and *devotional* use in public and private worship, 2) their *didactic* use in Christian education settings, and 3) their *artistic* use in paintings, drawings, statues, etc. Consequently, he often jumbles everybody together and implies that anyone who makes or uses any kind of representation of Jesus is an idolater. This is *not clear* from the second commandment.

Of course, it's very likely that Barnes feels that any educational or artistic use of pictures of Jesus inevitably *leads to* an idolatrous use of such representations. Maybe he believes that pictures of Jesus used in the classroom *tempt* (or actually *cause*) children and adults to violate the second commandment and so *worship* God falsely. But if he believes this, he does not explicitly argue for it anywhere in his pamphlet. Instead, in my judgment, he carelessly confuses worship, education, and art.

One must understand that by mingling these categories together the "clear direction" of the second commandment becomes rather murky. When you leave the activity of worship ("bowing down" and "serving") and enter into the spheres of education and art, you move away from the explicit concern of the second commandment. By failing to make the proper distinctions, Barnes obscures the real issues and collapses everything into the one category of idolatry.

After Barnes concludes the discussion of his "clear principle," he sums up with this logical deduction: "Since God is triune, this logically means that we are not to portray the Father, nor the Son, nor the Holy Spirit." No, not exactly. What Barnes ought to have said is: "Since God is triune, and the second commandment clearly forbids the *worship* of God by means of images, this logically means that we are not to *worship* the Father, or the Son, or the Holy Spirit by means of artistic representations."

Again, Barnes subtly confuses the categories. Have you ever wondered why God visually represented himself in the form of an enthroned man on Mt. Sinai? The elders of Israel "saw God" (Exod. 24.11). Or why the Holy Spirit was visually pictured in the form of a dove at Jesus' baptism? Luke 3:22 says, "The Holy Spirit descended in bodily form like a dove." If in fact all visual (even mental) images of any of the three Persons of the Godhead are idolatrous and dangerous, then why is the Holy Spirit *visualized* in the *bodily* form of a bird? Why did the elders of Israel *see* God seated on a throne? These are images (symbols, likenesses, etc.) of God! Surely anyone who personally witnessed these events saw an *image* of God, and likewise anyone who reads the stories today will form *mental images* of the God of Israel and Holy Spirit's descent in the form of a dove. Is it idolatrous to form such mental pictures when we read texts like this? Surely not. And if we can (and must) picture these representations of God in our mind's eye, may we not also paint or draw them as well?[3]

------

3. There may be some evidence to suggest that the meaning of the second commandment has been altered somewhat in the New Covenant. Deuteronomy 4:15-18 gives an historical rationale for the second commandment when it reminds the people that they "saw no form of Yahweh when Yahweh spoke" to them at Horeb (v. 15). But we don't live in the Old Covenant era. Did those who witnessed the inauguration of the New Covenant "see no form"? For the New Covenant believer, the question now becomes: since God has revealed himself in the bodily form of a man (1 John 1:1), may we make artistic representations of that form? Has the situation changed for us? The incarnation of the Second Person of the Godhead appears to have *altered* the redemptive historical situation. In the New Covenant God *did* speak to man by means of a visual form. We did see an image, a form, a likeness, when the incarnate Yahweh sat on a mountain and recapitulated the Ten Words (Matt. 5-7). It is precisely *not* an invisible God that the Apostles of

In summary, Barnes fails to establish the second

Jesus proclaim to us, but rather "that which was from the beginning, which we have heard, which we have *seen with our eyes*, which we have *looked upon*, and our hands have handled, even the Word of Life" (1 John 1:1). The Old Covenant revelation of Deuteronomy 4:15-18 must be interpreted in light of the New Covenant situation as explained in 1 John 1:1. It is now appropriate to artistically represent Yahweh as taking the visual, depictable form of a man. Here the Eastern Orthodox theologian John of Damascus is more sensitive to the redemptive historical context of the second commandment than are many of the Reformed. He argues that the interpretive context of Exodus 20:4-6 is Deuteronomy 4:15-18. That Old Covenant interpretive context has changed. God has become incarnate. This leads John of Damascus to assert: "I represent God, the Invisible One, not as invisible, but insofar as He has become visible for us by participation in flesh and blood." Times have changed, John of Damascus argues. In the light of 1 John 1:1ff. and *the incarnation of Yahweh*, the commandment must be applied to a new context, one in which Yahweh has appeared in the form of a man (Phil. 2:7, 8). John of Damascus may go too far in formulating his position so paradoxically ("the Invisible One. . . has become visible"), but it is certainly true that God has *revealed himself* differently in the New Covenant. Note well, that by acknowledging the accuracy of John of Damascus's insights here, I am not countenancing everything he has to say about icons. The Eastern Orthodox err in claiming that Jesus may now be worshiped and venerated by means of such representations, but they are correct when they argue that Jesus may be depicted as commandment as a clear principle prohibiting pictures of Jesus for purposes other than worship. His arguments from the second commandment are not convincing. The second commandment clearly forbids the crafting of any image for the purpose of "bowing down to" or "serving" it or serving God through it. This much is *clear* from the wording of the second commandment.

———————

a real human creature. There is a substantial difference between an icon and a picture. One is designed to link heaven and earth, while the other's purpose is to assist the memory in recalling an historical reality. On the redemptive-historical argument of the iconodules, see St. John of Damascus, *On the Divine Images*, trans. David Anderson (Crestwood, NY: St. Vladimir's Seminary Press, 1980), 16, 23, 25, 30; and John Meyendorf, *Byzantine Theology: Historical Trends & Doctrinal Themes* (New York: Fordham University Press, 1974), 45-46.

Accuracy, Imagination, and Art

Writing about art is like dancing about architecture.
—Anonymous

Next, we come to the heart of Barnes's argument against representations of Christ. He offers three arguments against them:

1. All pictures of Christ are necessarily inaccurate and dependent upon imagination.

2. Pictures of Christ are not only inaccurate, but they are a means of introducing much error concerning him.

3. Pictures of Christ necessarily dishonor him.

Before we examine each of these arguments in turn, it is important to note something significant about each of them. *All three are extra-Biblical arguments.* Although Barnes quotes many passages throughout his exposition of these three arguments, nevertheless, the arguments themselves are *philosophical* in nature. Don't overlook this point. Barnes may use Bible passages to explicate these arguments, but *the arguments themselves are not found articulated on the pages of Scripture.*

Argument #1
All Pictures of Christ are Necessarily Inaccurate and Dependent Upon Imagination.

Barnes considers this a weighty philosophical argument against pictures of Jesus. My initial response to the undeniable truth that all pictures of Christ are inaccurate and dependent upon the imagination is "So what?" The argument appears to be that any representation that is not completely accurate and independent of "imagination" is "falsehood and make-believe."[1] This is absurd. If representations and pictures must be free from all error and any imaginative influence from the artist, then all artistic representations that are, or have been, or will be, of anything whatsoever—they are all "falsehood and make-believe." Barnes's argument proves too much. It leads to the repudiation of all ar-

---

1. Barnes, 5.

tistic representation. Since this is a very popular argument against pictures of Jesus it is necessary that we examine this line of reasoning very closely.

First, if "inaccuracy" and "imagination" are the bugbears here, then all artistic representation of any real-life subjects are forbidden. Using Barnes's criteria, a watercolor portrait of my wife would be wrong. It would be necessarily inaccurate since *all artistic portraits must abstract from the complexity of the real thing* to enhance certain elements that the artist finds interesting. (In fact, this process of abstracting from life to enhance our understanding and appreciation of some aspect of life is part of the essence of the artistic endeavor.) Such a work of art would also be dependent upon the imagination of the artist since each particular artist always brings his own personality (imagination) to the creation of his work of art—even photographers and videographers! Thus, *Barnes's argument from "inaccuracy" and "imagination" is a speculative, extra-Biblical argument grounded in a radical misconception concerning the purpose of artistic representation.*

Second, Barnes points out correctly that no precise description has been handed down regarding the physical appearance of Jesus, but then he goes on to suggest that "slender hints" can be ascertained from the Scriptures about how Jesus looked. Well, which is it? If we have "slender hints," then we can form mental pictures, and if mental pictures, then physical representations. Referring to Isaiah 53:2, Barnes notes, "All that can be derived from this is that there seems to have been nothing majestic or striking in the physical appearance of the incarnate Word."[2] Well, here's a *partial* description. It at least gives the artist a *boundary*. Let's say that an artist were to depict Jesus passing through the fields with his disciples eating grain to illustrate a children's Sunday School handout on the Gospel of Mark—he would, for example, be forbidden by this Scripture (Isa. 53:2) to draw or paint Jesus as if he were some super-human being with unusual physical characteristics. Jesus looked like everybody else. He could even pass through the crowds without being recognized. The Pharisees had to get someone to identify him (Judas) even at the end of Jesus' three-year ministry among them! *The point is that we do know from the Scriptures that any representation of Christ must faithfully depict him as a normal human being.* At least as far as his physical characteristics are concerned, he was not something weird or out of the ordinary.

Even Barnes recognizes that the Bible *does* give *visual* descriptions, no matter how general, of Jesus' hu-

---

2. Barnes, 3.

man appearance. Barnes also cites John 8:57 to prove that Jesus' hard work during his three-year ministry had caused him to look older than he really was (a debatable inference). Granting for the sake of the argument the legitimacy of Barnes's interpretation, here is another partial *visual* description. A mental image necessarily follows! Again, assuming the accuracy of Barnes's interpretation of John 8:57, the Scriptures have given us a *visual* image and thereby established some real boundaries for artists. The direction from this passage: be careful not to depict him during his three-year ministry with the smooth-skinned complexion of a twenty-year-old man.

J. Marcellus Kik makes a similar point in his short pamphlet against pictures of Jesus: "Nowhere in the Bible, either in the Old Testament or New Testament, is there a physical description of Christ. Isn't that strange if God wanted us to use the picture of Christ in spreading the Gospel or in worship, that we are not told whether Christ was tall or short, fair or dark, light or dark hair, blue eyes or brown eyes."[3] Leaving aside the *physical* description of Jesus given by the Apostle John in Revalation 1:12-16, let us grant Kik's point.

---

3. J. Marcellus Kik, *Pictures of Christ* (Havertown, PA: New Covenant Publications, n.d.), 3.

Of course, there is no *physical* description given in the New Testament for the purpose of making a *portrait* of Christ. Nevertheless, there are many highly descriptive passages concerning the *historical* events of Jesus' life. The Bible does describe the historical encounters of the man Jesus. I am not arguing for *portraits* of Jesus but rather for artistic representations of the Bible-revealed historical acts of Jesus. In order to faithfully communicate the reality of such events no detailed anatomical description of Jesus is required.

Third, Barnes's criterion *rules out too much*. Barnes *overstates* the case when he makes his big point: "Christ has come in the flesh, but we have no real idea what he looked like."[4] No real idea? Sure we do. He looked like a *man*. He had all the common features of humanity: two eyes, a nose, a mouth, two arms and legs, etc. He was a male Jew about 30 years old, about five feet tall. He wasn't eight feet tall, nor did he weigh 300 pounds. We *do* have an idea of what he looked like. Barnes himself has already admitted as much!

Barnes, however, assuming that the sole purpose for which anyone might want to depict Jesus would be to provide an *accurate portrait*, reminds us that the Spirit has not told us how tall he was or what color eyes

----

4. Barnes, 4.

or hair he had. So what? Even if the Spirit did give us some of these physical characteristics listed by Barnes, would he be satisfied? Probably not. Barnes is looking for an *exhaustive* description. Nothing less, according to Barnes's logic, will enable the artist to depict Jesus. This is a sly move. Barnes knows that even if we had a hundred written pages devoted to a physical description of Jesus, *an artist would still have to interpret the data and fill in the gaps!* The artist would have to make the tricky transition from the written word to the visual image, and that would necessarily involve the artist's own imagination and talent. Therefore, according to Barnes's philosophical criteria, a picture of Jesus would never be allowed!

This call for *accuracy* is a wax nose. According to Barnes's argument, anything short of a comprehensive description would lead to inaccuracies and therefore be deceptive. But how could a *written* account ever provide such an exhaustively accurate picture? The very way in which Barnes has formulated his argument rules out *a priori* the very possibility of artistic depiction since it is impossible for *verbal* communication to provide exhaustively accurate *visual* information.

Let's follow the implications of Barnes's logic to its absurd conclusions. Barnes's principle is so rigorous that *it rules out as deceptive and dangerous all attempts to depict artistically any biblical character or scene what-soever!* Don't miss this. Barnes's argument, if consistently applied, must rule out any artistic representation of Peter or Paul. Since any picture of these two apostles will necessarily involve inaccuracies and imagination, therefore, any picture of them will be "falsehood and make believe." Away with all Sunday School material with pictures of Paul and Peter! And, for that matter, away with all pictures of all Biblical characters, cities, homes, animals. . . everything that contains inaccuracies! They are all "make-believe"!

Let me make sure you get my point. Using Barnes's argument, pictorial representation is ruled out not just for Jesus but for anyone or anything described in the Bible! After all, we're not *really* sure what any of the *disciples* looked like, and we *really* don't know *exactly* what their houses looked like, and we can't be sure that we can ever *accurately* recreate "authentic" first-century scenery. Therefore, using the logic Barnes as adapted, *all* pictures of first-century *people* and *situations* "are necessarily inaccurate and dependent upon imagination," which means, of course, they are dishonest, deceptive, and therefore forbidden.

Lest the reader think I am being unfair, remember that Barnes's argument thus far is a philosophical argument based on the supposed inaccuracy of all pictures of the human Jesus. This argument has nothing to do with the second commandment or even, as I hope to show, with the deity of Christ. When pushed to its logical implications it leads to absurd conclusions.

The Purpose of Art

Fourth, *Barnes misrepresents the purpose of art.* Barnes declares, "Under the inspiration of the Holy Spirit, the apostles simply did not see fit to describe the Lord for us. . . . The point remains: Christ has come in the flesh, but we have no real idea what he looked like".[5] Now admittedly, this would be an insurmountable obstacle to one who intended to depict Jesus *as he really looked.* Indeed, Barnes is seeking to make an airtight case against pictures of Jesus based on his argument against all artistic productions that are "inaccurate" and "imaginative." Since we don't have a comprehensive description of Jesus' humanity, all attempts to depict Jesus would necessarily be deceptive— "falsehood and make-believe," as Barnes puts it.

Now, this argument would be sound if the *purpose* for which every picture was drawn was to provide the viewer with an *accurate portrait* of the subject. Barnes fails to understand that abstracting from the subject

---

5. Barnes, 4.

matter (resulting in what he calls "falsehood" and "in-accuracies") as well as the imaginative participation of the artist (leading to what he labels "make-believe") are part of the essence of art.

All this talk of "falsehood," "make-believe," "authenticity," and what "He really looked like" betray Barnes's misunderstanding of the nature and purpose of art. No doubt Barnes would object to Rembrandt's *The Adoration of the Shepherds* since Christ is depicted there as a shining baby, literally suffusing all the faces of those who are gazing at him with a warm light. Veith is right when he notes that "Rembrandt is not simply showing what the Bethlehem stable looked like (actually, the Christ-child must have looked like any other baby); rather he is using his artistic medium *to proclaim the meaning of that event*. . . . [he] is not only illustrating Luke's Christmas story (Luke 2:8-20), but also John's: 'The True Light that gives light to every man was coming into the world' (John 1:9)."[6]

---

6. Gene Edward Veith, Jr., *State of the Arts: From Bazalel to Mapplethorpe* (Wheaton, Ill: Crossway Books, 1991), pp. 44, 45, emphasis mine. See W. A. Visser't Hooft, *Rembrandt and the Gospel* (London: SCM Press, 1957) for an interpretation of the meaning of the rays which sometimes surround Christ's head in some of Rembrandt's drawing. Visser't Hooft believes

Which artist ever self-consciously sought to depict Christ as he really looked? When has the *authentic representation of the physical appearance of Christ* ever been the stated or implied *intent* of an artist or of a Sunday School curriculum illustrator? Let us consider an artist who intends to depict a scene from Christ's life. What if the artist, in an attempt to isolate some characteristic of Christ's personality and capture something of the drama of an event in the life of Christ, were to paint a picture of Jesus summoning Matthew the tax collector (e.g., Caravaggio's *The Calling of St. Matthew*)? Must he hide Christ's face and body behind a door or a shadow because "we're not really sure what he looked like"? The face of Jesus is barely discernible in the darkened stern of the fishing boat in Rembrandt's *The Storm on the Sea of Galilee*. Is Rembrandt's point that we don't know what Jesus' face looked like? It is not likely.

Barnes himself refers to El Greco's painting of Christ cleansing the temple. He admits that the painting "brilliantly portrays the Lord's intensity, singleness of purpose, and holy power." Exactly. This was El Greco's purpose—*to artistically and imaginatively abstract*

---

that Rembrandt made use of such rays in a manner that broke with the stereotypical halos of Medieval and Renaissance religious art.

these qualities for us by portraying them on canvas so as to enhance our understanding and appreciation of the event.

Nevertheless, for Barnes that's not good enough. He asks "how authentic is it?" Does he mean "how authentic is the size, height, and facial appearance of Jesus as he appears in this painting?" What else could he mean? But El Greco never dreamed that he was recreating what Jesus *really* looked like, nor surely did he think that anyone with a whit of common sense would ever mistake his artistic representation for the "authentic" likeness of Christ. Again, Barnes seems to be unaware of the nature and purpose of art. Barnes labels these artistic portraits of Christ "falsehood" and "make-believe," as if in order to be "true" to the subject any artist must "authentically reproduce" (whatever that means!) a man's exact physiological features without any imaginative freedom. If this were so, then the only kind of morally permissible art would be video art! And even with this technology the medium and the "artist" wielding the camera are not entirely objective and invisible, so that we might rightly question even the "authenticity" and "objectivity" of video-taped presentations. (Neil Postman makes a very good case for the subjective and imaginative influence of the videographer in his book *How to Watch TV News.*[7])

J. Marcellus Kik boils it down to this: "How would you like it if someone who never saw you painted a picture and told everyone that it was a picture of you? Certainly you would resent it. And certainly Christ must resent all those counterfeit pictures of him." How would I like it? Well, that all depends. It depends on what the artist was trying to do. If the artist painted a *portrait* of me, one that had no resemblance whatsoever to what I really looked like, then I probably would resent it. But if the artist, in an attempt to remind people of my personal history, painted me in a pulpit preaching to a congregation of Christians, then why would I object—especially if there was no attention directed toward my facial or physical anatomy? Would such a picture, even though the artist had no direct knowledge of exactly what I looked like, be a "counterfeit"? Hardly. Should a picture of Moses standing over the Red Sea, his arm raised, the rod of God in hand, be judged a "counterfeit" just because we are not exactly sure what Moses looked like? No. The purpose of such

----

7. Neil Postman and Steve Powers, *How to Watch TV News* (New York: Penguin Books, 1992), see especially chapter 8, "The Bias of Language, The Bias of Pictures," 97-114.

a picture is to make us recall an historical event. Similarly, pictures of Jesus on the crest of a hill teaching a crowd of people seated on the green grass below him are meant to remind us of an *historical* event in the life of Jesus. Nothing more. Whether Jesus' physical constitution precisely and minutely corresponds to what he really looked like on that day is beside the point.

Can This Principle be Consistently Applied?

Fifth, Barnes's argument based on inaccuracy and imagination has even more problems. Does this prohibition include *any* representation of Jesus Christ whatsoever? Are we allowed to show his hands, his feet, or any other part of his body? Some Sunday School materials that purport to follow the no-pictures-of-Jesus-philosophy will often keep Jesus off the page, occasionally showing a hand or a foot. I have seen the back of Jesus portrayed as he teaches the crowds. Some will even allow a *faceless* body to appear on the page.

But how does this practice square with Barnes's argument? After all, we don't know for sure what his hands or feet may have looked like either, and any picture will necessarily be *inaccurate*, depending as it must on the artist's *imagination*. Would Jesus' hand really have looked like that? How can we be sure that his feet were really the size that the artist portrayed them?

Now, if someone retorts that my discussion of these incidental features of Jesus' anatomy deflects us from Barnes's main point, I would have to disagree. They are *precisely* the point, according to Barnes and the no-pictures-of-Jesus argument. Barnes's objection to a drawing of Jesus in a second-grade Sunday School class handout is that "we don't *really* know what he looks like, so how can we dare depict him." What does he mean? Does he mean that we're not sure whether he looked like a normal man or not? (Most illustrated children's story books depict Jesus as a normal man.) No, of course not. We know he was a normal looking man. That's not the issue. Barnes would no doubt respond, "No, it's not that we don't know whether he looked like a normal man or not—obviously he did! The real issue is whether or not he looked like *this* man that the artist has drawn in *this* cartoon." The question, then, for Barnes must be: Is *that* what Jesus *really* looked like? In other words, are the *incidentals* of Jesus' physiological body *accurately* portrayed—his height, weight, facial appearance, hair color, etc.?

Note carefully that the opponent of pictures of Jesus (using Barnes's first argument) objects to the *particular* face that this artist has given Jesus, to his muscular build, to the size of his nose, to the color of his hair, and so on. "How can we be sure?" our opponent asks. But I respond: why have these concerns about Jesus' *incidental* features (eyes, ears, nose, hair, etc.) been given such an important status? Why should Jesus' minor physical features be invested with such exalted significance?

Whether Jesus had a certain sized nose or a certain length of hair *is beside the point.* These are *incidental* features that are easily recognized as such. To fuss over the accuracy of such incidental features and suggest that *idolatry* is somehow involved borders on superstitious fastidiousness.

To warn children against viewing an illustration of the *face* of Jesus "because we're not sure what he really looked like" is completely beside the point. Why focus on the face? Why not warn them not to view Jesus' hands or feet? Why not warn them about Peter's or John's face? Again, we are back to the *purpose* of the particular picture of Jesus. *The Sunday School illustration merely wishes to convey to the children the truth that Jesus was a genuine man like the disciples*—if they even have such a weighty intention in mind at all! The artist seeks to abstract some historical event from the life of Christ and enhance our understanding of it through visual media. That kind of purpose does not demand absolute accuracy. This is a far cry from fashioning an image for the purpose of worshiping God through it. A child whose understanding of a particular event in the life of our Lord is enhanced through such a visual representation is not worshiping an image.

Thus, Barnes's argument *proves too much* on two counts. First, it would rule out all representations of Jesus or any part of Jesus whatsoever. Second, it holds out an impossible standard, since *no* artistic representation of *anyone* or *anything* is entirely accurate or free from the imaginative influence of the artist. As I have said already, according to the strict logic of this argument, no representations of anyone or anything would be allowed, since they would all to some extent partake of "falsehood" and "make-believe."

It's All in Your Imagination

A sixth point: It is important to recognize that Barnes's argument reduces to absurdity as we press it in another direction as well. It proves too much again, since it effectively rules out *all imaginative* and *artistic* representations of Jesus, both visual and *verbal*! *A preacher may not, on Barnes's principles, depict Jesus Christ verbally to his congregation using any imaginative, extra-Scriptural descriptions of him whatsoever.* He may not put any words in his mouth other than the precise ones which Jesus uttered. He may not describe Jesus in a way that powerfully calls up the visual imagination of the people.

If, for example, a preacher was preaching on Jesus praying in the Garden of Gethsemane or the crucifixion, then to *describe* Jesus' agony and even his physical sufferings *would necessarily call to mind mental images of Christ in his congregation*. And if mental images of Christ fill the minds of the congregation because the preacher has so artfully described the torments of Jesus, then he has introduced falsehood and make-believe into the minds of his congregation by imaginatively describing Jesus' situation so as to call forth mental images of Jesus' physical appearance. Therefore, the preacher is forbidden to skillfully use language as a means of describing Jesus (or Jesus' life or character) to his congregation. Thus, the principles articulated by Barnes lead to even more absurdities.

Seventh, laying aside for the moment the preacher's use of verbal artistry to conjure up pictures of Jesus, consider the Bible's own language. The Bible itself uses highly descriptive language to describe many events in the life of our Lord, even describing Jesus himself in many situations. Sure, we are not told incidentals about his physical appearance. Even so, how does one avoid *mental* images of Jesus weeping, of Jesus sweating blood, of Jesus' scarred hands and side, of a lamb seated on a throne, etc.?

Do you see? *Every* image the mind calls up as the Gospel stories are read will necessarily be *inaccurate* and mingled with our own *imagination*. The Christ you picture in your mind will not be the "authentic Christ." Again, we have no earthly idea what he *really* looked like! How do you know what size his hands were? How do you know for sure how big his side wound was? How then can you *accurately* picture him in your mind?

Here we have the same problem as before. No one in his right mind really believes that the mental picture he forms of Jesus standing with a woman by a well is *authentic*. When we hear this story we conceive of a real man standing with a real woman, and we visualize him speaking and drinking. That's all. No idolatry is intended, nor does any necessarily ensue from mental images of Gospel stories involving Jesus. Thus, Barnes's argument also logically rules out all *mental* images of Christ's humanity that result from *scriptural* descriptions as dangerous and wicked—images which cannot possibly be avoided, nor ought they be! On yet another count, then, Barnes's logic is found wanting.

Summary of the Critique
of Barnes's First Argument

Let's step back and summarize Barnes's first argument based on the inaccuracy of all pictures of Jesus. The absurdity of Barnes's inaccuracy argument, I think, is now clear. The purpose of a Sunday School handout that portrays Christ driving out the money changers from the temple is not to recreate an *accurate* picture of what Jesus really looked like. Nor is it to suggest any such thing to the children who benefit from this kind of visual, educational aid. It is not intended for, nor is it used as a *medium* through which to worship Jesus. Neither is it designed to capture or conjure the essence of Jesus' person or his divinity. It is merely an aid to teach children a Bible story. That's it. Period.

But now, our opponent may respond, "Don't you see!? You've given it all away. Jesus was not a normal man! He was a divine-human person. That's precisely why you cannot capture his essence in an artistic conception." Note well that the opponent has now shifted arguments. Realizing that his argument based on inaccuracy and imagination is unsound, our opponent has moved on to an entirely different argument. The argument now is not based on our inaccurate knowledge of Christ's physical appearance but concerns *the inability of an artistic representation to capture his divine nature.* We will answer this objection shortly.

The opponent may also move on to the argument that any representation of Jesus constitutes a dangerous *temptation* for some to worship Jesus through the medium of such a representation. In short, pictures of Jesus *may lead people into idolatry* and for that reason ought to be avoided. But this argument is also a new one, and one with which we will have to address.

I believe the above considerations effectively reduce Barnes's first argument, considered on its own merits, to absurdity. Again, it is imperative to point out that Barnes's first argument has nothing to do with the second commandment and nothing to do with idolatry. Nor is it, strictly speaking, a *biblical* argument. Although Barnes *utilizes* Bible passages to *illustrate* his argument at points, his polemic is not a Scriptural one, but one based on a certain (mistaken) conception of art as well as a flawed view of the intentions of artists and illustrators. Barnes presents us with a reasoned, *extra*-biblical argument. It is *philosophical*, not biblical. Unfortunately, as often as this very argument is repeated—and that in very solemn tones by some pastors and theologians—*it has been fallaciously assumed to be* a biblical argument. It is not even a cogent argument considered on its own merits.

A Picture Tells a Thousand Lies

. . . at one point I found myself standing before an oil of a horse that I figured was probably a self-portrait judging from the general execution . . .
—Peter De Vries

Argument #2
Pictures of Christ are not only inaccurate, but they are a means of introducing much error concerning him.

We turn now to Barnes's second argument against all representations of Jesus. Here again Barnes passionately denounces pictures of Jesus because they do not give us the "authentic Christ." It is important to realize that this "second" argument turns out to be little more than a restatement of the first with a focus on the errors that "inaccurate" portrayals of Christ necessarily produce. All the arguments we marshaled against his first argument apply to this one as well. A more accurate appraisal would see this section as an *illustration* of his first argument and not really a separate argument at all. In other words, although Barnes cites this as a second argument against pictures of Jesus, there is really very little difference between this argument and the one preceding it.

He contends specifically that the inaccurate and inauthentic pictures of Christ produced by any particular culture tend to recreate Christ after the image of that culture. "Hence we find," according to Barnes, "the Byzantine Christ, the Anglo-Saxon Christ, the African Christ, the hippie Christ, and so on—but none of them the authentic Christ."[1]

Hold on. Barnes uses very prejudicial language to describe how each culture depicts the physical appearance of Jesus. He charges that each culture "recreates him in its own image." Anyone familiar with the biblical language of the prophets will not miss the allusion to idolatry by Barnes. But is this really idolatrous? Isn't this "re-creation" rather innocent? Doesn't it have more to do with the *meaning* and *relevance* of Christ to each race and culture than it has to do with idolatry?

---

1. Barnes, 5.

Everyone knows that Jesus didn't look like a Chinese man, but the Chinese man is reminded of the universal application of Christ's work when he sees Christ depicted in "his own image." Everyone knows that Jesus didn't look like an Anglo-Saxon, but the Anglo-Saxon artist seeks to communicate something to Anglo-Saxons about the relevance of Jesus' character or life to Anglo-Saxons. How else could he depict him? Thus, the artistic depiction of Christ as a Chinese man or an Anglo-Saxon uncovers something of the *meaning* of the incarnation. The artist's purpose is not to recreate the *authentic* Christ (an impossible prospect, as we have seen), but *to enhance our understanding of the universal nature of the incarnation.*[2]

Barnes uses the adjective "much" to describe the error that attends pictures of Jesus. Again, as we pointed out with regard to Barnes's first argument, Barnes

---

2. I asked the question in this paragraph, "How else could the artist depict him?" and the obvious answer is that he could represent him as a first century Jewish man! Even though I might understand and sympathize with an artist's motivation, I'm not sure it's really all that helpful. If we are avoiding *portraits* altogether (as I argue we must), then any historical scene depicting Christ ought to seek to be true to the facts. My point in this paragraph, though, is to insist that such racial-sensitive pictures of Jesus are not necessarily idolatrous.

thinks that *incidental* features such as racial or ethnic appearance (skin color, size of nose, etc.) constitute "much" error. Barnes has merely asserted his claim, not proven it. How do pictures of Jesus that introduce cultural or ethnic features in Jesus' facial or bodily appearance become the source of "much" error? What evil consequences follow? Barnes does not say. Even if someone mistakenly believes that Jesus looked like the people of his ethnic lineage, to what great theological or moral error has he fallen prey?

Argument #3
Pictures of Jesus necessarily dishonor him.

Building on the first two arguments, Barnes now marshals what he believes is the most devastating argument of all. Barnes thinks that he has now reached the crux of the argument against those who maintain that the human nature of Christ justifies pictorial representations. He calls this "the most serious point" of all.[3] Here he points out that the second commandment is violated even by those who intend merely to use pictures of Jesus as aids to devotion or as educational helps. Barnes's argument builds on three primary premises:

———————————

3. Barnes, 5.

1. The second commandment forbids not merely the *worshiping* of images but also the *making* of them as well.

2. Every picture of Christ leaves out the fullness of his glory and therefore dishonors him.

3. To attempt to depict the human nature of Christ without the divine nature dangerously separates the two natures of Christ, presenting at best a "half Christ."

Before going on to critique this argument, I must distance myself from what Barnes implies with regard to the use of pictures of Jesus for *devotional* purposes. Barnes lumps together two uses of pictures of Jesus that ought not to be confused: 1) pictures of Jesus used as an *aid to devotion*, and 2) pictures of Jesus used as a teaching or educational aid.[4]

To gaze at a picture of Jesus as an *aid to devotion* is nothing more than using it for *private worship*. This is expressly forbidden by the second commandment. In this booklet, I am *not* advocating that "portraits" of Christ be used as devotional helps.[5] (I am not promot-

---

4. Barnes, 5, 6.

5. I am trying to be as precise as I can with my language. By

ing "portraits" at all, but pictorial depictions of historical events in the life of Christ as well as artistic interpretations of his life.) By illegitimately mingling these two uses, Barnes prejudices the case against proper educational and artistic uses. I can agree with Barnes's last paragraph in this section if he would remove the references to teaching.[6] It is true that a believer who has a picture of Jesus in his house to use in conjunction

---

"aid to worship" I mean something akin to an icon—something that functions as a medium through which to communicate with or conjure up God. If we use the word "aid" in a more general sense as meaning "help" or "assistance," then there is a sense in which a picture or even a symbol (a cross) in one's home can function legitimately as an "aid to devotion." A painting of Jesus rebuking a Pharisee on a crowded Jerusalem street, for example, might serve to remind us of Jesus' righteous hatred of religious Phariseeism. A drawing (on the opposite wall) of Jesus raising Lazarus from the dead might call to mind that Jesus is the resurrection and the life. Seeing these pictures aids the Christian by reminding him of historical events in Jesus' life and of the meaning of those events. They are in some sense "aids to devotion." Are they idolatrous? No. Why not? Would we be tempted to bow down and worship Jesus through these artistic works? Hardly. They depict Christ in Bible-based historical settings.

6. Barnes, 8.

with private worship or in his church to use as an aid to public worship violates the express commandment of God not to *worship* him through the medium of any *artistic rendition of himself.* Barnes rightly insists: "In such a case, the picture has not become an aid to devotion or understanding, but a bondage. It ought to be destroyed."[7] Well, at least it ought to be removed from the environment of worship if it is functioning as a medium of communication with Jesus.

Let us now return to Barnes's "most serious point": that God is necessarily dishonored by *all* images of Jesus, regardless of their use or intended purpose. Consider Barnes's first premise: the second commandment "forbids not only the *worshiping* of images but also the *making* of them."[8] Is this really the case? Does the second commandment forbid the making of images *without regard for their intended use*? Please note that Barnes does *not* seek to ground his opinion *exegetically*; he merely asserts it. But such a contention cannot be maintained from the language of the second commandment itself. The text of the second command-

---

7. Barnes, 8.

8. Barnes, 6.

ment does not support Barnes's interpretation. Consider again the words of the second commandment:

> You shall not make for yourself a carved image, or any likeness of anything that is in heaven above, or that is in the earth beneath, or that is in the water under the earth; you shall not bow down to them nor serve them. For I, Yahweh your God, am a jealous God, visiting the iniquity of the fathers on the children to the third and fourth generations of those who hate Me, but showing mercy to thousands, to those who love Me and keep My commandments (Exod. 20:4-6).

If Barnes wishes to maintain that the first part of the commandment (You shall not make for yourself a carved image, or any likeness of anything that is in heaven above, or that is in the earth beneath, or that is in the water under the earth) is grammatically and logically distinct from the second (you shall not bow down to them nor serve them), then he is forced to take the first part as an absolute prohibition of all artistic representation of anything whatsoever regardless of the intended use. Therefore, if the commandment forbids anything, using Barnes's logic, it forbids everything, not merely the making of all representations of God, but also the making of all representations of anything whatsoever "in heaven above, or on the earth beneath."

Furthermore, the commandment *alone* does not, as Barnes insists, forbid all representations of God. The commandment is not explicitly worded so as to forbid representations of God. It does not say, "Thou shalt not make any image or likeness of God." Rather, it forbids making an image of anything at all *in creation*. The reason for this manner of wording is because the first prohibition of the commandment is explained by the second prohibition: no image or likeness of anything created (birds, beasts, trees, etc.) may be made by man to be used as a medium for worshiping God. God will not be worshiped through the medium of an image or picture of anything in creation. Thus, the second clause *modifies* the meaning of the first.

This understanding of the text can be confirmed by checking any of the orthodox exegetical commentaries on Exodus. One example will suffice. The Dutch Reformed commentator W. H. Gispen comments, "The intent of verse 4 is thus further clarified by the prohibition: 'you shall not bow down to them or worship them.' This is the basis for the statement that the second commandment concerns the cultus."[9]

---

9. W. H. Gispen, *Bible Students Commentary—Exodus*, trans.

What of Barnes's second premise in this argument: that every picture of Christ leaves out the fullness of his glory and therefore dishonors him? He claims that the second commandment's "sweeping prohibition is based on the truth that *all* representations of God dishonor him. This is equally true of the person of Christ."[10] What shall we make of this argument? Does the text of the commandment give this rationale? No. Does the commandment itself ground the prohibition against worshiping images on the truth "that all representations of God dishonor him"? No. This is the product of Barnes's theologizing. He may be right, but *the text of the second commandment* does not give this rationale for the prohibition of the worship of images.

Ed van der Mass (Grand Rapids: Zondervan, 1982) 191. See also James B. Jordan's tape series *Expository Lectures on Exodus* (Biblical Horizons, 1992), lectures #37-40. Jordan's translation brings out the genuine force of the commandment: "You shall not make for yourself a carving; to wit: any similitude of what is in the heavens above or on the earth beneath or in the waters under the earth, you shall not prostrate to them, and you shall not serve them." The commandment forbids *prostrating* ourselves before or serving human *artifacts* as liturgical *devices* of worship.

10. Barnes, 6.

First, is it true that all representations of God necessarily dishonor him? Although it may sound very pious, as a sweeping universal it is quite mistaken. *Please note that this is not the stated reason for the prohibition of images in the language of the second commandment.* God does not explain the rationale for the prohibition the way Barnes does. The text does not articulate this reason. Barnes thinks this is the reason. But is it?

Do all representations of God necessarily dishonor him? Let me state the question a little differently. Do all *images* of God dishonor him? Is God nowhere represented (symbolized) by his creation? Of course. Man is an image (representation) of God. We can learn about God by observing humans who are made in his image. Given the fact that man does not *fully* reveal God, that humanity does not (to use Barnes's own words) portray God in the full glory of his deity, does not at all imply that mankind's "imaging" of God is dishonoring to him! Furthermore, in addition to humanity's *special* representation of God, many other parts of creation *generally* symbolize (picture) God to mankind. The Bible nowhere explicitly affirms that God is automatically dishonored by representations.[11]

---

11. On the way in which man and the world reflects (images) the glory of God, see James B. Jordan, *Through New Eyes: De-*

What it does emphatically affirm is that man must not make an image with the express purpose of worshiping or serving it either as a god or as a representation of God (Isa. 44:8-20).

In 1974, the Reformed Presbyterian Church of North America (RPCNA) published a symposium called *The Biblical Doctrine of Worship*. It was the fruit of the Synod's Committee on Worship, and its purpose was to expound the Reformed tradition's "Regulative Principle of Worship" as well as to establish exegetically and defend the same as a genuine Scriptural principle. The result is a series of essays that have become the standard apology for the "hard core" Reformed doctrine of worship. Yet even here, the authors who deal with the second commandment recognize that *the language of the commandment cannot be pressed beyond its intent*. The commandment forbidding the making of images must not be understood too rigorously. In his essay entitled "Implication of Exodus 20:3-6 for the Doctrine of Worship," Donald Weilersbacher correctly notes that having mental conceptions or making physical representations of Jesus *for any other purpose than worship* are considerations that lie "outside of the scope

---

veloping a Biblical View of the World (Brentwood, TN: Wolgemuth & Hyatt, 1988).

of this directive and therefore must be decided upon by other considerations."[12]

Let us pursue this issue of mental images a bit further since it is relevant to the discussion of Barnes's third argument. If we cannot depict Jesus artistically, then may we mentally picture him when we hear one of the Gospel stories about him? Would this be a violation of the second commandment? All of the arguments marshaled by Barnes apply with equal force in prohibiting mental pictures of the humanity of Christ when we read the Gospel stories. If all images of God necessarily dishonor him, then mental pictures of Jesus must also dishonor him. So according to Barnes, all mental images of the humanity of Christ would also be dishonoring to him and actually be the source for the introduction of much error concerning him.

This position might appear to be confirmed by the *Westminster Larger Catechism's* exposition of the sins forbidden by the second commandment in Question 109: "The sins forbidden in the second commandment are . . . the making [of] any representation of God, of all, or of any of the three Persons, either inwardly in our mind, or outwardly in any kind of image or likeness of any creature whatsoever. . . ."

------

12. *The Biblical Doctrine of Worship*, 22.

Two points should be made about this interpretation of the second commandment. First, the issue appears to be the making of images of the *deity* of God, whether Father, Son, or Holy Spirit. The incarnation of the Son, and his taking upon himself a fully human, and therefore depictable image, does not appear to enter the horizon of discourse.

Second, one must note carefully, according to the wording and intent of the entire answer, that the purpose of the Catechism is to forbid the *worship* of both physical and mental images of the First, Second, or Third Person of the Godhead. Allow me to quote Weilersbacher's discussion of the meaning of the Catechism's answer:

> But if the intent is to say that we may not have a mental image of what Jesus was like at his birth or crucifixion, or that there may be absolutely no visible representations of Jesus in his humanity, then such an interpretation goes beyond the scope of Scripture. Certainly, anyone who attempts to worship Jesus by, to, or through a two or three dimensional representation is sinning. But the mere existence of such a representation

is not in itself a sin, as long as it is treated with no more respect or reverence than any work of art.[13]

Weilersbacher goes on to make a very telling point.

Whenever we preach that the soldiers nailed Jesus to the cross at Calvary, we automatically convey a mental image of what was happening; and such a mental image is not sin! Moreover, if Jesus had waited until 1973 to begin his earthly ministry, journalists and photographers would have flocked to his side. There would have been in the morning newspapers pictures of his cleansing the temple, healing the sick, casting out demons, and raising the dead. Furthermore, these pictures would not in themselves have constituted sin. Only if one were to worship the picture, giving it a reverence that is not proper, would a person be guilty of idolatry.[14]

Is it desirable or even possible consciously to seek to avoid framing mental pictures of Christ as we read the record of his life in the Gospels? Must we, when we read the story of Jesus passing through the grain

---

13. Weilersbacher, 22.

14. Ibid.

fields with his disciples (Mark 2:23-28), inwardly picture twelve disciples walking through the field with an empty space where Jesus should be? Are we forbidden a mental image of Jesus driving out the moneychangers from the temple with a whip? Must we consciously erase any notion we might have of the man Jesus from such a mental image, with the result that we picture a whip gliding through the air apparently unsupported? What about Revelation 1? Can anyone possibly read this passage without creating a mental image of the glorified Christ? Isn't that just the purpose of such descriptive imagery? And if not, how much more seductive can language be? Is the Lord tempting us to idolatrous mental images by inspiring such graphic descriptions?

If you will grant the inevitability, even the beneficence, of mental images that arise from a story well told, then it's a short step to putting your mental image on canvas in order to illustrate and enhance the meaning of the story.

Weilersbacher concludes his 1973 essay with the suggestion that it would be wise for the Reformed church to restudy the matter and then decide whether having a mental image of Jesus or a visible representation of his true humanity does indeed constitute sin. The "mental images" issue has been thoroughly examined by John K. Lashell in his dissertation "Imaginary

Ideas of Christ: A Scottish-American Debate."[15] Lashell concludes that the application of the prohibitions against idolatry to making mental images is unwarranted and therefore mental images are not prohibited by Scripture. Unfortunately, the "physical representation" issue still dogs many parts of the Reformed church and needs fresh examination.

---

15. John K. Lashell, "Imaginary Ideas of Christ: A Scottish-American Debate," (Ph.D. diss., Westminster Theological Seminary, 1985).

We Have Seen His Glory

God made the world that he might communicate, and the creature receive, his glory. . . . God's glorifying himself comes from one cause, viz. the overflowing of God's internal glory, or an inclination in God to cause his internal glory to flow out ad extra.
—Jonathan Edwards

Let us return now to Barnes's principal argument—that all pictures of Christ necessarily dishonor him. We have examined his first premise, that the second commandment forbids all representations of God, and found it wanting. We are in the process of examining Barnes's second premise: *every picture of Christ leaves out the fullness of his glory and therefore dishonors him.* "Artists cannot portray Christ in the full glory of his deity, so they are generally forced to attempt to portray him only in the humility of his manhood."[1]

It is certainly true that artists cannot portray Christ in the full glory of his deity, but does it follow that they are "forced" to limit their representation to his humanity? Hardly. The assumption is that any representation of God's glory that falls short of *comprehensively* depicting the fullness of the glory of God necessarily compromises and devalues God's glory. Is that really the case? God himself has never *fully* revealed his glory to man. But does this imply that he has revealed *nothing* of his glory? Or that his glory is incommunicable?

Indeed we might argue that it is impossible for God to reveal his glory *fully* to his finite, created beings. At the very least it would seem to be impossible for his creatures to assimilate fully the fullness of God's glory. But we all know from the Scriptures that God *has* revealed his glory to man. The Scriptures even inform us that men have *seen* God's glory. Consider the following passages:

> And in the morning *you shall see the glory of Yahweh*; for he hears your complaints against Yahweh (Exod. 16:7)

---

1. Barnes, 6.

Now it came to pass, as Aaron spoke to the whole congregation of the children of Israel, that they looked toward the wilderness, and behold, *the glory of Yahweh appeared in the cloud* (Exod. 16:10).

The sight of the glory of Yahweh was like a consuming fire on the top of the mountain in the eyes of the children of Israel (Exod. 24:17).

Now *the glory of Yahweh appeared* in the tabernacle of meeting before all the children of Israel (Num. 14:10).

. . . because all these men *who have seen my glory* (Num. 14:22).

And Korah gathered all the congregation against them at the door of the tabernacle of meeting. *Then the glory of Yahweh appeared to all the congregation* (Num. 16:19).

So Moses and Aaron went from the presence of the assembly to the door of the tabernacle of meeting, and they fell on their faces. *And the glory of Yahweh appeared to them.* (Num. 20:6).

Like the appearance of a rainbow in a cloud on a rainy day, so was the appearance of the brightness all around it. *This was the appearance of the likeness of the glory of Yahweh. So when I saw it,* I

> fell on my face, and I heard a voice of One speaking (Ezek. 1:28).

> And the Word became flesh and dwelt among us, and *we beheld his glory*, the glory as of the only begotten of the Father, full of grace and truth (John 1:14).

> This beginning of signs Jesus did in Cana of Galilee, and *manifested his glory*; and his disciples believed in him (John 2:11).

It would appear, then, that for Barnes to insist on the fullness of God's glory as a prerequisite for artistic representation goes beyond the biblical record. Just because an artist does not have the fullness of God's glory at his disposal does not at all prohibit him from artistically communicating that portion of God's glory to which he does have access. Surely the glorious environment of the tabernacle and temple were designed to communicate God's glory to the people.

Does God ever reveal his glory to man without veiling the comprehensive fullness of his glory? To ask the question is to answer it. Not on this side of heaven. If all communications and representations of God's glory this side of heaven are necessarily partial and limited, how can this fact be used to argue against a partial representation of Jesus' glory?

If the Second Person of the Godhead did, in fact, humble himself so as to veil the fullness of his glory from man, then may we not depict the meaning of that event artistically in order to communicate that historical fact? Surely the incarnation partially hid the Son's glory for a time (Phil. 2:5-8).

Barnes says, "Pictures necessarily detract from his divine glory."[2] Did his depictable humanity necessarily *detract* from his divine glory? His glory was *veiled*, but did it detract from it? Did the disciples see the fullness of the Second Person's glory when they gazed at Jesus during his three-year ministry? No. But even so, John tells us, "the Word became flesh and dwelt among us, and *we have seen his glory*, glory as of the only Son from the Father, full of grace and truth" (John 1:14).

Barnes illustrates this principle by an incident in the life of Amy Carmichael. I find Carmichael's comments confusing at best, an example of religious enthusiasm at worst. Does the Holy Spirit give us some kind of mental vision of what Jesus looks like? What else can Carmichael mean when she laments that the pictures of Jesus that people gave to her orphans turned out to be so "much less beautiful than the one the Holy Spirit

---

2.   Barnes, 6.

had shown [the children]."[3] Whatever does she mean? That the Holy Spirit reveals beautiful mental images of Jesus to minds of those who have no artistic representations? This appears to be exactly what she means. She tells a story of a little girl who received a picture of the boy Jesus in the temple. The little girl wept with disappointment when she saw the picture of Jesus. "I thought he was far more beautiful than that!" the girl said. But what does this prove, *besides the fact that this little girl had already formed a mental image of Jesus' physical humanity*—an *idolatrous* image on Barnes's premises! She then critiques the artistic depiction she received by means of the false standard of her own imaginative image of Jesus (one which the Holy Spirit supposedly "revealed" to her!).

Barnes then concludes, "We may safely leave the blessed Spirit to show to the people to whom we speak, something 'far more beautiful than that.'"[4] What does *this* mean? If we understand Barnes's statement in terms of the Carmichael story just told, then it can mean nothing less than that the Holy Spirit shows people mental images of Jesus' physical appearance

---

3. Barnes, 7.

4. Barnes, 7.

and that these are more beautiful than that of any artist. The vague and pious sounding language of Barnes may fool some, but as an argument against pictures of Jesus it lacks any force whatsoever. It even appears to advocate or at least condone some sort of private, inner revelation.

Next Barnes appeals to the Puritan divine John Owen in order to bolster his argument that the divine glory of Christ is debased and compromised when anything other than the fullness of Jesus' glory is communicated—something which cannot be captured artistically in any picture of Jesus. Owen claims that the glory of Christ is "glory absolutely of another kind and nature than that of any other creature whatever." This being the case, he warns, "We may see hence the *vanity* as well as the *idolatry* of them who would represent Christ in glory as the object of our adoration in pictures and images."[5] Barnes then quotes a long section in which Owen disparages all images of Jesus as "fancies of superstitious persons," "as having a resemblance of glory," and as "delusions."

What shall we make of Owen's comments? First, the context of Owen's discussion has to do with *worship*, especially the liturgical and devotional use of

---

5. Barnes, 7.

images of Jesus. This much is obvious even from the relatively short section quoted by Barnes. Owen refers to those who would "represent Christ in glory *as the object of our adoration*." Once again, we have an argument against the use of pictures of Jesus as a medium of worship and adoration, but not one against all representations of Jesus regardless of their intended use.

Second, Owen, in context, is speaking of the *glorified* Christ. This at least leaves open the question of whether Christ in his humiliation, during the time in which he veiled his glory, might not be depicted. Owen's arguments are directed against the use of pictures and statues of the glorified Christ as an aid to worship and devotion, not about the possibility of artistically communicating, for example, the meaning of some event in Jesus' life outside of the context of worship and devotion.

Third, Owen's arguments against the possibility of representing the glory of Christ are based on the assumption, common to much of Reformed theological discussion on worship, that the finite cannot capture the infinite (*finitum non est capax infiniti*). Carlos M. N. Eires argues in his *Against the Idols: The Reformation of Worship From Erasmus to Calvin* that the acceptance of this philosophical principle pushed the Reformation and post-Reformation church into more and more radical liturgical tendencies—tendencies which led to white-washed churches, the abandonment of all "material" props in worship, and the acceptance of a false standard of "spiritual worship" understood as that which is opposed to "physical" worship.[6]

Does it necessarily follow that if any glory is possessed by the creation, that God's glory is diminished? Is the creation barred from reflecting the glory of God? Is creation's communication of God's glory comprehensive? Hardly. Is creation therefore a dangerous detraction from the fullness of God's divine glory? Or does God manifest his glory in varying degrees by means of his creation? It may be true that the finite cannot *capture* the infinite, but the real question is can it *reveal* the infinite?[7]

Fourth, building on what has been said above, we would ask Owen whether it is possible then to repre-

---

6. Carlos M. N. Eires, *Against the Idols: The Reformation of Worship From Erasmus to Calvin* (Cambridge: Cambridge University Press, 1988).

7. Calvin surely thought that the creation was a genuine theater of God's glory, though not comprehensively. See Susan E. Schreiner, *The Theater of His Glory: Nature and the Natural Order in the Thought of John Calvin* (Durham, N.C.: The Labyrinth Press, 1991).

sent Christ *verbally* to people if in fact any diminution of the fullness of Christ's glory in communicating the nature of his Person necessarily detracts from his glory and leads to "delusions." Does not language just as much as art carry certain inherent limitations? If an artist cannot capture the glory of Christ, then neither can a writer! Both must necessarily abstract from the whole of Christ's glory in order to communicate some aspect of it to others. If such an abstraction does not constitute idolatry in literature, then why must it in the visual arts? We can apply Owen's arguments to sermons just as well as we can to paintings. The pastor after all is an artist of sorts. He must choose a portion of Christ's glory to communicate to his hearers. He must then imaginatively and artistically "display" a portion of Christ's glory to his congregation.

And one more point: John Owen's arguments can just as well be applied to the *visual* imagery of Christ's glorified humanity revealed in Revelation 1. The idea once again is that if we cannot represent Christ's glory comprehensively, then it is a sin to seek to represent it at all. Any *partial* picture is necessarily an erroneous picture, one that detracts from his glory. But is Revelation 1: 12-16 a revelation of the *fullness* of Christ's glory? Or is it a *true* but *partial* revelation of his glory? In answer to this someone may say that the book of Revelation, after all, is Scripture! So it is. That is precisely the point. The philosophical argument used by Barnes and Owen that any partial communication of Christ's glory always amounts to a sinful diminution of his glory does not seem to be a concern to the Apostle John as he provides for us a visual image of the glorified Christ (Rev. 1:12-16).

The argument we have been examining is not based on our inaccurate knowledge of Christ's physical appearance but concerns the inability of an artistic representation to capture the glory of the divine nature. Is the fact that an artist cannot capture the fullness of the divine glory a liability? Christ's humanity itself did not (and does not) capture or communicate the fullness of God's glory, nor did it comprehensively communicate the essence of his divinity. This is a very important theological point. The incarnation was not an *incarceration* of the Second Person of the Trinity. *His divinity was not confined to nor circumscribed by his humanity.* Jesus *added* a human nature to his divine person. Strictly speaking, Barnes's argument would rule out Christ's appearance as a man since anyone who might see him during his earthly ministry would have been unable to *see* the fullness of the glory of the divine nature.

Let's ponder this idea. The Scriptures seem to indicate that the invisible God himself was made visible in the incarnation of the Son. In some sense, God was pictured *through* the humanity of Christ. Not the *fullness* of the deity, of course. The human nature of Jesus did not *capture* the invisible essence of God, but it did reveal it somehow. Think about these passages:

> "The Word became flesh and dwelt among us, and we *beheld* his glory, the glory as of the only begotten of the Father. . ." (John 1:14).

> The Son is "the brightness of his glory, and *the express image of his person*. . ." (Heb. 1:3).

> "That which is from the beginning, which we have heard, *which we have seen with our eyes*, which we have looked upon, and our hands have handled, concerning the Word of Life. . ." (1 John 1:1).

These passages are all carefully worded and occur in very theological sections of the New Testament. They do not say merely that eyewitnesses saw Jesus' *human* nature, but that the divine nature was somehow represented or pictured in the incarnation. After all, God had depicted himself to man in the Old Testament, usually by means of a human form (cf. Exod. 24:9-11; Judg. 13:15-23; etc.). Man himself is an *image* of God, and therefore a fit vehicle for God's revelation of himself. The incarnation was the last and great *image* of God. I am not suggesting that these passages teach that God's invisible essence was made visible to man. Or that God's nature was somehow *captured* by means of these pictures. What these passages suggest is that God has indeed revealed himself in the form of visual imagery. Another example that comes to mind is the visual representation of the Holy Spirit at Jesus' baptism. The Holy Spirit is *pictured* as a dove (Matt. 4:16, "He saw the Spirit of God descending like a dove"). All these passages suggest that it is not improper for us to use visual symbols, especially the symbol of the man Jesus, to represent God.[8]

---

8. All of these pictures or representations of God are only symbols. It would be helpful to keep in mind that even words are symbols. The letters of the alphabet are symbols. The word "God" is a symbol. It is not a sin to represent God in any of the ways that he has symbolized himself in the Bible. The sin is to break the second commandment by *bowing* down to or *serving* the symbol. If a stained-glass window depicting the baptism of Jesus reminded us of the biblical story, then it would function merely as a symbol. There would be no violation of the second commandment. But if one stood at the window *gazing* at the dove above Jesus' head, seeking to communicate with the Holy Spirit by means of the artwork, this would be idolatry. We should recognize that *words also can become idols*. Writing the

name JESUS on a card, setting it up, and staring at it in order to communicate with God would also violate the second commandment.

The Two Natures of Christ

. . . the mantle of our flesh is the mantle taken by God himself at his incarnation. Most glorious mantle—no ermine, no purple, no cloth of gold, no robe of angelic light can match it.
—Thomas Howard

Barnes has another twist to his third argument. He claims that to attempt to depict the human nature of Christ without the divine nature dangerously separates the two natures of Christ, presenting at best a "half Christ." Barnes claims that all who seek to represent Christ "must leave aside the exalted Christ . . . and restrict themselves to conjectures as to his human form."[1] Here Barnes again slips in his polemic against the "conjectures" of artists concerning his physical appearance.

---

1. Barnes, 6.

I'm not sure what Barnes is trying to get at here. Leaving aside his comment on "conjectures" (which we have adequately examined already), we have the following: "leaving aside the exalted Christ . . . restrict themselves . . . as to his human form." Is the exalted Christ not a fully depictable human form? Why must we abandon any artistic or educational representation of the exalted Christ? Does Barnes believe that the exalted Christ has now been stripped of his assumed created nature? This would be heresy. In heaven the Son retains his union with his material human substance, confined to space and time. Glorified yes, but nevertheless still a fully human created nature. I don't think Barnes intends to convey such an error. But could it not be that here we discover dangerous semi-docetic tendencies in Barnes's position?

I am honestly confused when Barnes goes on to assert, "But Scripture allows no such separation between the two natures of Christ."[2] What is the "separation" to which Barnes is referring? Presumably, Barnes is accusing those who want to artistically represent the humanity of Christ with erroneously separating the deity and humanity of Christ. But in context Barnes has just described the difference between "the exalted Christ"

---

2. Barnes, 6.

and "his human form." Who is guilty of separating the person of Christ? The exalted Christ is the God-man. The exalted Christ continues to subsist in his human form. Barnes's accusation of an undue separation is confusing. How am I guilty of separating the natures of Christ when I insist on the truth of his assumption of a depictable, created, human nature? How am I guilty of separating the natures of Christ when I draw a picture of Jesus teaching the people on a hillside? If Barnes replies, "You leave out the divine nature in your representation!" then I respond, "Precisely, since his divine nature cannot be depicted!"[3]

In what way does an artist who depicts Christ's humanity "separate" his humanity from his deity? How? I honestly don't see it. I can see how such a representation will clearly highlight Christ's depictable humanity. Anyone viewing such a picture will be able to *distinguish* between the visible form of the humanity of Jesus and the invisible Divinity of the Second Person of the Godhead which is not visible to the eye of man. But

---

3. It is important to make the necessary distinctions. Jesus' humanity was a *revelation* of the invisible God. The incarnation itself did not *capture* the essence of the invisible God but revealed him. God was not *incarcerated* in Jesus' human nature, He became incarnate.

how does this encourage a separation or a severing of the two natures?

Indeed, one might argue that Barnes's position tends to *mingle* the two natures together and to endanger the real, physical humanity of Jesus Christ. If the Scriptures do not allow a separation of the two natures, then neither do they allow any mixture or confusion of the two natures such that their respective natures lose their distinctive properties. To refuse to depict Christ in his human form means to confuse the human and the divine natures, which was the error of Eutychianism.

Although Barnes does not refer to it, consider R. L. Dabney's comments on images of Jesus in his *Systematic Theology*:

> As to the picturing and worshiping of the man Jesus, the delineation of his Human person has more shadow of reason [that is, appears to be more reasonable-J.M.], because He is incarnate. But there is no portrait or description of Christ which is authentic. If there was, He is now, when glorified, wholly unlike it. Chiefly, an image could only represent his humanity, as distinguished from his divinity; and the former, thus abstracted, is no *proper object of worship*. The use

of the crucifix in worship, therefore, tendeth to evil.[4]

Dabney's entire discussion revolves around the question of *worship*—whether it is acceptable to *worship* Jesus through the medium of an artistic representation. He is concerned about the use of *portraits* and *crucifixes* in private and public worship. Nevertheless, he mingles extra-biblical philosophical arguments (the concern over the "authentic" portrait) with overblown language. Is Christ's glorified body "wholly unlike" the body of his humiliation? Dabney laments that when Jesus is depicted, Christ's humanity is "abstracted" from his deity. What could that mean? And why is it necessarily *bad*? When I preach a sermon on Jesus' crucifixion, I *abstract* this event from the rest of the life and work of Jesus. Is there a problem with that? Well, Dabney is concerned that no one *worship* the humanity of Christ severed from his divinity. He believes that images of Jesus used for worship encourage this very

---

4. Robert L. Dabney, *Lectures in Systematic Theology* (Grand Rapids: Baker Book House, [1871] 1985), 362, emphasis mine. Once again, the argument based on authenticity is the major premise of Dabney's argument against pictures of Jesus. We have already argued that the question of authenticity is not really relevant.

error. Whether this is true or not, one cannot help but note that the entire discussion revolves around the *liturgical* and *devotional* use of images of Jesus; the question of whether Jesus may be artistically depicted for other uses does not enter into the horizon of Dabney's concern.[5]

The creed of the fourth ecumenical council at Chalcedon (A.D. 451) remains the classic statement of the theology of the two natures of Christ. The Council sought to chart a biblical course that would avoid the errors of Eutyches (confusing the two natures) as well as that of Nestorius (dividing the two natures.) The resulting formula has remained the benchmark for all subsequent Christological discussions.

> Therefore, following the holy fathers, we all with one accord teach men to acknowledge one and the same Son, our Lord Jesus Christ, at once complete in Godhead and complete in manhood, truly God and truly man, consisting also of a reasonable soul and body; of one substance

---

5. John Frame's critique of arguments that depend upon derogatory conceptions of abstraction deserves to be consulted by those who may not see my point; see *Doctrine of the Knowledge of God* (Phillipsburg, N.J.: Presbyterian and Reformed Publishing Company, 1987), 169-191.

with the Father as regards his Godhead, and at the same time of one substance with us as regards his manhood; like us in all respects, apart from sin; as regards his Godhead, begotten of the Father before all ages, but yet as regards his manhood begotten, for us men and for our salvation, of Mary the Virgin, the Godbearer; one and the same Christ, Son, Lord, Only-Begotten, recognized in two natures, without confusion, without change, without division, without separation; the distinction of natures being in no way annulled by the union, but rather the characteristics of each nature being preserved and coming together to form one person and subsistence, not as parted or separated into two persons, but one and the same Son and Only-begotten God the Word, Lord Jesus Christ; even as the prophets from earliest times spoke of him, and our Lord Jesus Christ himself taught us, and the creed of the fathers has handed down to us.[6]

If the one Christ is both God and man, then he must be both depictable and undepictable. We attribute both the created manhood and the uncreated

---

6. Gerald Bray, *Creeds, Councils, and Christ* (Leicester, England: Inter-Varsity Press, 1984), 162.

divine nature to the one Person of Christ. Opponents argue that to depict Jesus is to separate his human and divine natures because a picture of Jesus can only portray his human nature, while his divine nature remains impossible to depict. Of course, his divine nature is impossible to depict! In the strict sense of the word, his divine nature was impossible to see during Jesus' earthly ministry. No halo or aura surrounded the incarnate Christ! No one could have known merely by looking at him that he was theanthropic in his ontological constitution. The divine nature was (and is) not depictable.

My question, then, to those who argue against pictures of Jesus today on the grounds that such pictures presuppose or encourage a heretical division of Christ since they cannot *picture* the divine nature of Christ: If no one in the first century could have *seen* the invisible essence of God by merely looking at Jesus, did his historical presence itself encourage a division of the natures? Surely not. Since no one can ever see or depict the fullness of the divine nature, how can it be argued against those who believe in pictures of Jesus that such representations are wrong because they leave out the divine nature? The invisible divine essence was left out of the visual impression during Jesus' ministry! If Jesus' depictable humanity did not lead to the separation of his divine and human natures while he lived on earth, why should historical pictures of his life on earth necessarily divide his natures?

A picture of Jesus is not an attempt to depict the invisible Godhead but the material, created form that the Second Person of the Trinity, the Son of God, *irrevocably* assumed at his incarnation. Jesus' human nature did not lose its physical, finite properties when the person of the Son of God united himself to it, nor did he jettison his humanity when he was glorified and ascended. His ascended, human nature remained timebound, circumscribed by space, and fully depictable.

More important distinctions need to be made. Not even Jesus' human nature is exhaustively depictable. When I look at my mother, I see her outward appearance, but not her soul (or spirit, depending how you slice the pie of human existence). So there is a sense in which human nature itself is not exhaustively depictable. Nevertheless, that doesn't keep us from looking at each other! Nor does it keep us from artistically representing human beings. We understand when we look at such an artistic representation that it is symbolic. We all know that there is more to a human being than outward appearance. When I refer to Jesus' depictable humanity, I mean that his humanity was the created medium through which the Son chose to reveal himself. That nature is depictable in its outward appearance.

It was precisely the outward appearance that was the vehicle for God's revelation of his glory in the incarnation (John 1:14).

That our Lord Jesus Christ was and is *vere homo* as well as *vere Deus* constitutes one of the most fundamental confessional articles of Christendom. We are not necessarily safeguarding the humanity of Christ by allowing pictorial representations for didactic purposes—as if the defense of Jesus' humanity ultimately depended in some way on the pictures we make. Not at all. But pictures of Jesus do guard against the Christological *errors* of docetism and gnosticism, both of which, to put it mildly, depreciate the genuine material humanity of Christ. Pictures of Jesus will not in any sense *guarantee* the orthodox doctrine of his full humanity. Rather, they are a *defense* against these errors.

Pictures of Jesus are salutary, for example, in training young children about the Gospel stories: teachers can effectively illustrate biblical stories through the use of visual aids depicting various historical scenes. If a scene that purports to illustrate the story of Jesus feeding the five thousand contains representations of the disciples and the crowds, but does not contain any representation of Jesus, then a possible implication to be drawn is that Jesus was not a real man. Of course, *one* such picture will likely have no such effect on children, but if week after week, year after year, children continue to see the disciples, the Pharisees, and other men and women visually depicted, and *never* see Jesus at all, the danger becomes acute. Was Jesus really a true man? Was he a ghost? Was his body invisible? Did it shine? Did he look like a superman? Did the disciples see him? Did he even have a physical body? Was it able to be depicted? Was he weird looking? Wasn't he a real human being?

What I'm saying is that a picture of Jesus constitutes, in effect, a *confession* of the incarnation in space-time history. If such a pictorial confession is absent from certain artistic and educational contexts, an alternative confession, namely, that Jesus did not have the same kind of material body as other men depicted, becomes a lively option for the student.

The Ambiguity
of Church History

*To give an accurate description of what has never occurred
is the inalienable privilege and proper occupation of the
historian.*
—Oscar Wilde

For the next four or five pages of his pamphlet Barnes
attempts to marshal the testimony of the historical
church against those who would depict Christ's humanity. This portion of the pamphlet is particularly
weak. First, almost every citation or example Barnes
can find concerns the question of the liturgical and
devotional use of images or icons of Jesus. Second, the
history of the church is a mixed bag even on the question of the suitability of images of Jesus in worship!
One can amass all kinds of quotations against the use
of images from the eighth century iconoclasts to the

sixteenth century Reformers, but what does it prove? I could pile up references to those who argued *for* images, but what would that really solve? This is not an issue that can be solved by counting historical noses as Barnes leads us to believe.

The Pre–Constantinian Church: Pictures, But No Veneration

The early church evidence is particularly sketchy, even though Barnes writes as if the early church uniformly and unequivocally forbade all pictures of Jesus. Even as early as the eighth century, during the iconoclastic controversy, both sides could claim that they had the testimony of the ancient church on their side. Both sides collated testimonies from the early Latin and Greek Church fathers to prove their point. But Barnes is quite sure that the pre-Constantinian church was purified of all pictures of Jesus. He claims that in the post-Constantinian church "attitudes changed," "new and broader views" were more readily accepted, and "the church apparently came to accept more readily images of Christ." The evidence he presents is very slim indeed.

Against Barnes's contention that the pre-Constantinian was *uniform* in its denunciation of pictures of Jesus, consider any modern scholarly work on Christian art. I will refer to the recent *Encyclopedia of Early Christianity*, edited by Everett Ferguson.[1] In Paul Corby Finney's article "Art" (97-103) he refers to the "extensive remains of pre-Constantinian art in the many wall and ceiling paintings that survive in the oldest nuclei of the Roman Catacombs." In these Jesus is often depicted as the shepherd carrying a sheep or with his arms outstretched as a gesture symbolizing the gathering of his saints together for worship. Similar images of Jesus can be found in baptisteries and on sarcophagi. Finney does refer to an explosion of Christian art and iconography in the Constantinian and post-Constantinian era; but there apparently was no massive philosophical and theological change of mind with regard to propriety of images of Jesus as Barnes suggests, even though Barnes is correct to point out that the post-Constantinian church did increasingly advocate images of Jesus as aids to worship.[2]

---

1. Everett Ferguson, *Encyclopedia of Early Christianity* (New York: Garland, 1990).

2. H. W. Jansen's comments are appropriate: "Compared to painting and architecture, sculpture played a secondary role in Early Christian art. The biblical prohibition of graven images was thought to apply with particular force to large cult statues, the idols worshiped in pagan temples, so that religious sculp-

Barnes's citation of art historian Michael Gough to the effect that the pre-Constantinian representations are limited to a few historical episodes and that the passion and crucifixion of Christ are never depicted proves only that the development of the luxury of Christian art remained stunted until the church achieved more freedom. Gough's comments do not "verify" that the pictures of Jesus were universally condemned in the early church, but rather that very few scenes in the life of Christ were used in their art. The fact that the passion and crucifixion were not represented is beside the

---

ture, in order to avoid the taint of idolatry, had to eschew life-sized representations of the human figure. It thus developed from the very start in an antimonumental direction: away from the spatial depth and massive scale of Graeco-Roman sculpture toward shallow, small-scale forms and facelike surface decoration," *History of Art: A Survey of the Major Visual Arts from the Dawn of History to the Present Day* (Prentice-Hall & Harry N. Abrams, 1962), 166. The sarcophagus of Junius Bassus (A.D. 359) illustrates Jansen's point: a richly carved front, divided into 10 square compartments, shows a mixture of biblical scenes, such as the sacrifice of Isaac, the misery of Job, Daniel in the lion's den, Christ before Pontius Pilate, Christ's entry into Jerusalem, and Christ enthroned in heaven between Peter and Paul. These images are clearly illustrative of scriptural truths. They witness to the non-idolatrous use of pictures of Jesus in the early church.

point. The point is that there were pictures of Jesus in other contexts.[3]

Nevertheless, Barnes calls some pre-Constantinian witnesses. His first witness is Irenaeus, the bishop of Lyons (c. 115 - c. 202). Barnes notes that one of the arguments Irenaeus used against the Gnostics was that "They also possess images, some of them painted, and others formed from different kinds of material; while they maintain that a likeness of Christ was made by Pilate at that time when Jesus lived among them." Barnes then *illogically* concludes: "Portrayals of Christ, whether painted or carved, were seen as a Gnostic peculiarity, and a result of heathen influence."[4] But neither of these conclusions necessarily follow from Irenaeus' attack on Gnosticism. Irenaeus does not say that the idea of pic-

---

3. Paul Corby Finney, *The Invisible God: The Earliest Christians on Art* (New York: Oxford, 1994), insists that historians have misinterpreted the pre-Constantinian Christian understanding and use of art. He argues that even while attacking Greek polytheistic and pornographic art, the archeological evidence indicates that the early Christians were quite interested in symbolic and artistic representation. One can pursue the many photographs in Finney's latest book and see early Christian depictions of Jesus.

4. Barnes, 8.

tures of Christ derived from pagan influence, nor does it follow that Irenaeus was claiming that *only* the Gnostics had images of Jesus. What he was saying was that the Gnostics had statues and images of Jesus *which they claimed to have acquired secretly from a representation passed down from Pilate*. Barnes presses Irenaeus to say much more than he actually said. Barnes is reading too much into Irenaeus' simple statement.

This can be confirmed if we go back to the text of Irenaeus' statement and quote a larger portion of his comments in context. We then see that Irenaeus had the *worship* of these images in mind when he attacked the Gnostics. Here is what follows immediately after the quotation made by Barnes:

> They *crown* these images and *set them up* along with images of the philosophers of the world, that is to say, with images of Pythagoras, and Plato, and Aristotle, and the rest. They also have other means of *venerating* these images, after the same manner of the Gentiles.[5]

This puts a different light on Irenaeus' quotation. Irenaeus is not attacking the Gnostics because they

---

5. Irenaeus, *Against Heresies*, 1.25.6, emphasis mine.

used representations of Christ to teach their children about the life of Jesus; nor is he refuting their use of artistic portrayals of Christ; but rather, he is condemning their violation of the second commandment. The Gnostics *set up* these images for the purpose of *venerating* them.

What of Barnes's reference to Eusebius? Again, Barnes presses Eusebius' words in a direction alien to his genuine concern. Although Eusebius' intent has been distorted by the eighth century iconoclasts who used Eusebius to justify their condemnation of icons, Eusebius' real purpose was to warn the emperor Constantine's half-sister Constantia against the belief that *authentic portraits* of Jesus can be obtained or made. There were heretics in the third and fourth centuries who believed that a genuine portrait of Jesus had been passed down. He queries Constantia, "I do not know what has impelled you to command that an image of our Savior be drawn. Which image of Christ do you want? Is it a true and unchangeable one, *portraying his countenance truly*?" Consider the emphasized words. Eusebius warns against the folly of obtaining "portraits" of Jesus which supposedly portray his "countenance truly."

In addition to this, surely it is pertinent to point out that Eusebius held an erroneous view of the incarnation of our Lord, denying that the union of the divine and human natures was permanent. Eusebius believed that after Christ's glorification the Son of God shed the human form, thereby ceasing to exist in the realm of material reality; or to be more accurate, he believed that the humanity of Christ was transmuted and mingled with the divine nature upon his ascension. In the same letter Eusebius assures us, "the flesh of Christ has now been confused with the divinity." Thus, Eusebius denied that the glorified person of Christ retained his fully human, describable body. This heretical notion seems to have influenced his rejection of all images of the man Jesus Christ. They were a relic of a bygone historical episode in the drama of redemption, Christ is no more to be contemplated as fully human. So even if Eusebius did prohibit all pictures of Jesus, he did so because of a flawed, heretical theology of the Person of Christ.[6]

------

6. See the discussions of Eusebius in John Meyendorf, *Christ in Eastern Thought* (Crestwood, N.Y.: St. Vladimir's Seminary Press, 1987), 176-177, 189; and Jaroslav Pelikan, *The Christian Tradition: A History of the Development of Doctrine*, vol. 2, *The Spirit of Eastern Christendom (600-1700)* (Chicago: The University of Chicago Press, 1974), 101-102.

I am not arguing that the early church used images of Jesus in their worship as icons. I don't think they did. I believe that they had a much more biblical and reserved viewpoint on the use of images of Jesus than the post-Constantinian church. I do not, however, believe that the evidence indicates that they forbade all images of Jesus regardless of their use. The walls of the catacombs, baptisteries, and the relief sculptures on their sarcophagi testify otherwise. To suggest that the early church had views similar to those held by Barnes and that they uniformly objected to the artistic and educational use of representations of Jesus is too fantastic to believe given the scanty evidence that we possess.

The Reformation & Post–Reformation Attitude toward Pictures of Jesus

I heartily agree with Barnes's repudiation of the Byzantine and Medieval abuse of icons and images in worship. Surely the reformers were right to reject all such violations of the second commandment. But I will return to the questions I asked in the first few pages of this essay. Did questions about the appropriateness of pictures of God or Christ in *art and education* enter into the discussions of the sixteenth and seventeenth century Reformed theologians?[7] Even though many of their modern spiritual progeny have overextended the Reformers' attacks on images *in worship* and misapplied them to art and education, doesn't it remain true that our Reformed forefathers principally assailed the *liturgical* use of such representations? Where are the unambiguous polemics against the non-liturgical uses of pictures of Jesus?[8] They simply are not there.

---

7. See Sergiusz Michalski, *The Reformation and the Visual Arts: The Protestant Image Question in Western and Eastern Europe* (London and New York: Routledge, 1993).

8. John H. Leith summarizes the attitude of the Reformers to the visual arts in *Introduction to the Reformed Tradition*, rev. ed. (Atlanta: John Knox Press, 1981), 201ff. Leith reminds us that the Reformers drank deep of the humanist world-view which placed an enormous amount of confidence in the power of written and spoken communication. Most of the Reformers, therefore, were not convinced that art is an effective medium of communication and teaching. I am not suggesting (and neither is Leith) that the Reformers were wrong in seeking to restore the central place of preaching in the worship of the church. I do think, however, that many of them lacked the balance that was required in order to restore verbal communication without at the same time abandoning the importance of visual symbolism. See Carlos M. N. Eires, *Against the Idols: The Reformation of Worship From Erasmus to Calvin* (Cambridge: Cambridge Uni-

Luther's attitude toward ecclesiastical art is well-known. He condemned the radical iconoclasm of some of his followers and allowed for the use of artwork in the sanctuary as long as it did not interfere with the biblical message of Christ. He forbade the use of images of Mary as well as statues of legendary saints but allowed for such sanctuary decorations as crucifixes and other paintings and stained-glass windows that depicted historical biblical events. Luther also encouraged the production of art in general culture as well. Luther's friend and godfather of his children, Lucas Cranach, was quite an accomplished artist. His painting, *The Repose in Egypt*, is a down-to-earth representation of the Holy Family resting during their flight from Herod to Egypt. Veith comments: "The biblical figures here look like real people, not stylized symbols. Joseph is a doughty German carpenter, his hat in his hand. Mary is a peasant woman. Jesus is an actual baby, squirming in his mother's arms. They are located, not in a transcendent realm signified by beaten gold, but in a startling, realistic and detailed natural landscape."[9]

---

versity Press, 1988) for an in-depth discussion of this very issue.

9. Veith, 62.

What about the other continental Reformers, especially Calvin? It's well known that Calvin rejected Luther's practice of using images of Jesus in the environment of worship.[10] Calvin utterly rejects the creation and use of all images of anything whatsoever as aids to worship.[11] He also repudiates all attempts to capture the divine nature through artistry regardless of its intended purpose.[12] Thus, Calvin's views on the

---

10. See John Calvin, *Institutes of the Christian Religion*, ed. John T. McNeill, trans. Ford Lewis Battles (Philadelphia: Westminster, 1960), 2 vols., 1.11.1-15. The reader should note carefully that Calvin's arguments are marshaled against *the use of images for worship*. He is constantly referring to images being "set up," "honored," "carnally venerated," "worshiped," and "erected" in the church.

11. John Calvin, *Commentary on the Four Last Books of Moses*, trans. Charles Bingham (Grand Rapids: Baker Book House, [1852] 1981), vol. 1, 106ff. This is Calvin's exposition of Exodus 20:4-6, the second commandment. Calvin's entire discussion revolves around the liturgical and devotional use of images of God in worship.

12. John Calvin, *Calvin's Ecclesiastical Advice*, trans. Mary Beaty and Benjamin Farley (Louisville, Kentucky: Westminster/John Knox Press, 1991), 76-80. This is a translation of a letter refuting the inquisitor Matthew Horris, who had attempted to defend the fashioning of images of the divine nature. Calvin says,

lawfulness of images in the environment of corporate worship and for use as aids to private devotion are clear: such practices are gross violations of the second commandment.

But having reminded the reader of Calvin's clear stand against idolatry, the question remains: Did Calvin also repudiate the making of representations of Jesus for artistic or educational purposes? The answer to this question is difficult to establish if for no other reason than the fact that Calvin did not address this issue. We know that he had a positive view of the nature and purpose of art.[13] He says in the *Institutes*, "Sculpture and painting are gifts of God."[14] But as far as ever addressing the issue of pictures of Jesus in art or general culture, I have not been able to find any place where

---

". . . anyone who tries to capture the majesty of God, as given in the [biblical] visions, will falsify it."

13. The two summary essays in *Calvinus Reformator: His Contribution to Theology, Church and Society* (South Africa: Potchefstroom University for Christian Higher Education, 1982), 287-316, establish the fact that Calvin sought to liberate art from the bondage of the Roman Catholic Church and free artists to glorify God through their artwork. The essays make no mention of pictures of Jesus.

14. Calvin, *Institutes*, 1.11.12.

Calvin unambiguously condemns it. He may not have ever spoken to the issue at all. But his French disciples, in what has been called "The Golden Age of Calvinism in France" did apply themselves to the arts. Pierre Courthial compiles a list of sculptors, architects, and artists during the period. Among others, he mentions Jean Goujon (c. 1507-63) who created the bas-relief called the *Entombment of Christ* that now resides in the Louvre. He was also responsible for *The Good Shepherd,* "a sculptured wood panel embellishing a door at the Church of Saint-Maclou, in Rouen."[15]

What did the other Reformers (Zwingli, Bucer, etc.) say about this issue? What did the continental post-Reformation theologians think? What did the British Reformers and post-Reformation theologians say about pictures of Jesus? There are some indications that the views of Reformed theologians on this question were not as uniform as Barnes would lead us to believe.

In 1530 Bucer wrote one of the most important iconoclastic tracts, *Das Einigerlei Bild,* to justify the

---

15. Pierre Courthial, "The Golden Age of Calvinism in France, 1533-1633," trans. Jonathan Jack, in W. Stanford Reid, ed. *John Calvin: His Influence in the Western World* (Grand Rapids: Zondervan, 1982), 89.

destruction of liturgical images at Strasbourg. The treatise, however, does not condemn all uses of images, but allows for a legitimate place for images as long as they were not venerated.[16]

In his *The Stripping of the Altars*, Eamon Duffy notes: "Even in Zwingli's Zurich the stained-glass windows had been allowed to stand: no one had ever seriously suggested that the people knelt before images in windows to venerate them."[17] According to Caiger-Smith, although the seductive religious imagery of the Roman church was enthusiastically effaced, the early Anglican and Puritan churches often replaced these with mural paintings. These paintings were more abstract, and supposedly less susceptible to idolatrous abuse. They were "for the most part irreproachable, emblematic, or moral themes, such as Moses and Aaron with the commandments, or figures of Time and Death, incapable of arousing old, idolatrous attrac-

---

16. See M. Ashton's discussion of Bucer's book in *England's Iconoclasts* (London: Oxford, 1988), 203-210.

17. Eamon Duffy, *The Stripping of the Altars: Traditional Religion in England, 1400-1458* (New Haven and London: Yale University Press, 1992), 451.

tions."[18] These may not be pictures of Jesus per se, but they were artistic murals that decorated the inside of churches! It would probably shock most modern "Puritans" to learn that some of their forefathers decorated the environment of worship like this.

The fact that the Reformers and Puritans seldom (if ever) discussed the issue of making representations of Christ in art and education really leaves the one who would argue from the Puritans and Calvinistic Reformers without much relevant data. This fact is even more astounding when we consider how prominent and abundant artistic representations of Christ were in the sixteenth and seventeenth centuries. The works of the seventeenth century artist Rembrandt never (as far as I have found) received the condemnation from the Dutch Reformed community we would expect if they held to such a rigid, comprehensive prohibition as we are led to believe by many like Barnes today. Visser't Hooft carefully outlines Rembrandt's relationship to the Reformed community in Holland as well as the criticism leveled against his life and work, but not once

---

18. A. Caiger-Smith, *English Medieval Mural Paintings* (Oxford: Oxford University Press, 1963), 113.

does he cite any criticism of Rembrandt's use of images of Jesus in his work.[19]

Does the Westminster Confession clearly forbid pictures of Jesus outside of the context of worship? Of course, Barnes quotes the entire answer of the Westminster Larger Catechism Question 109, "What are the sins forbidden in the second commandment" as evidence that the Divines rejected all representations of Jesus. The answer, however, as we noted earlier does not clearly and unambiguously condemn all pictures of Jesus that might be used for non-devotional and non-liturgical uses. Since the Westminster Larger Catechism is the product of British post-Reformation Reformed theologians, is it not appropriate to ask if the artistic and educational uses of pictures of Jesus were even an issue to them?

The question, for example, of the exact meaning of the Westminster standards *in their historical context* on the question of the non-liturgical, non-devotional use of pictures of Jesus remains to be historically investigated. What variety of opinion, if any, was held by the Divines on this issue? Did the question of the artistic and educational usage of images of Jesus ever even arise? We know that the question of the *liturgical* use of im-

---

19. Visser 't Hooft, *Rembrandt*, 31-41, 60-70.

ages was a highly charged issue at that time. But was the use of images for *artistic* and *educational* purposes also at stake? My basic inquiry here is an *historical* one: Did the Westminster Divines hold different views on this subject so that the end product of their deliberations was a consensus of what was held in common? And if so, could this be the reason why the Westminster standards do not clearly forbid representations of Jesus' humanity in art and education? Given the fact that the Confession and Catechisms are the products of the deliberation of *committees* and an *assembly*, and therefore must be interpreted as *consensus* documents, I am inclined to interpret ambiguity in these documents as significant. There is no *explicit* condemnation of artistic representations of Jesus in the Westminster standards.

All things considered, I remain cautious about some of my historical judgments, particularly those having to do with the Reformation and post-Reformation posture toward pictures of Jesus for art and education. I will remain tentative about my conclusions simply because questions about the appropriateness of pictures of God or Christ in *art and education* do not seem to have been the preeminent issue with sixteenth and seventeenth century Reformed theologians. Even though many of their modern spiritual progeny have overextended the Reformer's attacks on images *in worship* and misapplied them to art and education, our Reformed forefathers principally assailed the *liturgical* use of such representations—unambiguous references to non-liturgical uses of pictures of Jesus have not yet been uncovered.[20]

---

20. Obviously, more could be said about the development of the Puritan suspicion toward art in general. Even though the Reformed continental tradition could be suspicious of the visual arts in the church, the arts were not despised in the wider culture. On the English Reformers' attitude toward art, see John Phillips, *The Reformation of Images: Destruction of Art in England*, 1535-1660 (Berkeley, 1973). There is some evidence to suggest that the Puritan antipathy toward art was fueled in part by social factors. W.R. Jones argues in "Lollards and Images: The Defense of Religious Art in Late Medieval England," *Journal of the History of Ideas* 34 (1973), that the antagonism displayed by the Lollards and their spiritual children toward art arose partly from the antipathy toward the upper-class privilege of artistic leisure (11). This is why the English iconoclastic movement met with such popular support. Recall the ease with which King Henry stripped the monasteries clean of all religious objects. Jones also argues that the visual arts dropped out of ecclesiastical life because of the influence of the pietistic, individualistic, moralistic, anti-sacramental orientation of the Lollard tradition (9).

Maybe, then, we can ascertain something of the Continental and English Puritan posture toward depicting Christ in art and education by examining the art of the period, especially the art sanctioned by Reformed theologians and churches. Where is the art "sanctioned" by Reformed theologians and churches, you ask? Well, many of the commentaries, theologies, and translations published by Reformed men often opened with a decorative cover page, what is called a frontispiece. Did these artistic cover pages ever contain images or pictures of Jesus? Well, yes, as a matter of fact, they did.

Some of the volumes published by the Calvin Translation Society in the nineteenth century contain facsimiles of the original artistic title pages (frontispieces) of some of Calvin's works. For example, the translation of Calvin's *Commentary on the Book of Psalms* [21] is preceded by a frontispiece attached to the original French version of 1563. It is a picture of a man kneeling by a tree. Out of the clouds two hands are extended. One with a sickle slices branches off of the tree and the other is grasping a branch newly plucked

---

21. John Calvin, *Commentary on the Book of Psalms*, vol. 1, trans. Arthur Golding (Grand Rapids: Baker Book House, [1571] 1981), xxiv.

from the same tree. Do these hands symbolically depict God? Or do they represent angelic harvesters? Probably the latter, but the image is unclear, and we might even think dangerous. Didn't Calvin know that these kinds of images could easily lead simple people astray?

We have an even more explicit image, symbolic of Christ himself, displayed on the cover of Calvin's Latin *Commentary on Jeremiah*.[22] On the titlepage of the Latin publication (1589) there is a very large anchor straddled by the letters "IC" (IHSOUS CHRISTUS abbreviated). The top of the anchor is shaped like a cross, and around the anchor and "cross" a serpent is coiled. Two hands grasp the anchor's shaft from the clouds. Here the image clearly refers to Jesus Christ. The image of Christ depicted as a serpent derives from John 3:14 ("And as Moses lifted up the serpent in the wilderness, even so must the Son of Man be lifted up.") Didn't the post-Reformation scholars and theologians know that to represent Christ artistically like this was a violation of the second commandment?

Now, of course, with these two examples I have not uncovered an actual drawing of Jesus the man, but they

---

22. John Calvin, *Commentaries on the Book of the Prophet Jeremiah and the Lamentations*, trans. John Owen (Grand Rapids: Baker Book House, [1850] 1981).

are in fact intended to be "images" of Jesus. Remember, the second commandment, if it is interpreted as forbidding all humanly crafted images of God whatsoever, not only forbids realistic pictures of Jesus but all images of him whatsoever. After all, the Israelites pictured Yahweh symbolically as a calf (Exod. 24) and thereby violated the second commandment. There's more, however.

I have a photocopy of the Arthur Golding's English translation of the *Sermons of John Calvin on Deuteronomy* in my library. The title page for this translation contains the date A.D. 1583. This is, of course, about 20 years after the death of Calvin, so we obviously cannot hold Calvin responsible for its artistic contents. Nevertheless, neither can we believe that Golding would present such a theological and exegetical gem as Calvin's sermons on Deuteronomy, containing all of Calvin's repeated blasts against idolatry, to his fellow Reformed pastors and theologians with a title page that most of them would interpret as idolatrous. The ministers of Geneva even wrote the preface. In the center of the cover page is a picture of Jesus, the Good Shepherd, carrying a lamb on his shoulders. An image of Jesus as the Good Shepherd.

Huldreich Zwingli's (1484-1531) antipathy to the use of images in worship is well known.[23] The Zurich Reformer was, in fact, an image smasher. He and his followers gutted the churches of Zurich of all art whatsoever. His views respecting the use of images in worship are made quite clear in his *Commentary on True and False Religion* (1525). Nevertheless, the title page of his pamphlet *A Clear Instruction Concerning the Lord's Supper* has four panels of illustrations. The top panel depicts the way in which the supper was conducted in the newly reformed churches of Zurich. The left panel pictures the Israelites collecting manna. But the right and bottom panels are most interesting. The first is a drawing of Christ feeding the five thousand. The bottom panel shows the Last Supper. In both of these drawings Jesus is easily identifiable as the man who has a shining halo around his head. Apparently, the fiery Zwingli, who would not tolerate any images

---

23. See Charles Garside, *Zwingli and the Arts* (New Haven: Yale University Press, 1966). Upon seeing a newly white-washed sanctuary in Zurich, Zwingli proclaimed it "positively luminous" (160). Such a statement is itself a symbolic, visual interpretation.

in the environment of worship, had no problem with pictures of Christ for *illustrative purposes*. [24]

Moreover, consider the title page of the 1611 King James Bible. It is an elaborate drawing depicting the transition from Old Covenant to New Covenant. In the center of the page on top is the Tetragrammaton (the name "YHWH" in Hebrew). Below that is a lamb (Jesus Christ) carrying a cross! An angel directs the pen of Moses on the left (Heb. 2:2), and a lion (an image of Jesus Christ, Rev. 5:5) sits over the left shoulder of the representative author of the New Testament. On the page in the center is a stone altar with a bound and bleeding lamb (another image of Jesus) sprawled on top. Apparently, the Reformed Puritans had no problem with the use of these images. Now, granted, they would never have dreamed of displaying these images in the environment of worship, that is, on the walls or windows of the church, but apparently they had no problem with their use on an artistic cover for their Bible.[25]

---

24. Hans J. Hillerbrand, ed., *The Reformation* (Grand Rapids: Baker Book House, 1978), 151.

25. If anyone cares to examine this cover page, one can find it in Leland Ryken, *Worldly Saints: The Puritans as They Really Were* (Grand Rapids: Zondervan, 1986), 136.

I spent a few hours looking for these five examples. If I had the time I no doubt could find many more. But the point is clear. On the one hand, Calvin saw no inconsistency with prohibiting images in the environment of liturgical worship while at the same time using them for artistic purposes. Apparently, many of the post-Reformation Reformed theologians and some of the Puritans felt the same way.

Conclusion

Let me conclude my analysis with a brief explanation of my position by summing up some of the conclusions that we have reached here and there throughout the essay. Barnes's arguments from Scripture, theology, and history are unconvincing and strained. The second commandment does not clearly forbid pictures of Jesus for non-devotional uses. He fails to establish his conclusion that all representations of Jesus, without regard to their intended use, ought to be prohibited.

My position is as follows:

1) Christians are forbidden by the second commandment to *worship* God through the medium of humanly crafted representations of God or his creation.

2) I am convinced that the commandment also prohibits all idolatrous attempts to conjure or manipulate or communicate with God using such images. This

rules out the use of icons or icon-like images in private or public worship.

3) I am not advocating the presence of *portrait* representations of Jesus in the environment of Lord's Day worship. They would constitute a great temptation to those who are weak or ignorant. Thus, I believe that the environment in which pictures will be used must also be carefully considered.

4) I cannot see any good reason to commend what are erroneously called "portraits" of Jesus, such as the famous American "portrait" by Sallmon. These kinds of pictures are invitations to devotional abuse. Gary North makes the following telling comments in his commentary on the second commandment:

> Now that God has come in the flesh and has manifested himself among men, it is legitimate to represent God by making representations of Jesus Christ. How can such statues or paintings be kept from becoming magical talismans, amulets, or icons? *By placing the representations in a Bible-revealed historical setting.*
>
> We do not know what Jesus looked like. We know that he was sufficiently nondescript that the Jews paid Judas to identify him. So we

cannot legitimately represent Jesus apart from recognizable historical settings from the Bible. The historical setting is the identifying mark of who the image represents. It points also to a *one-time only* event in man's history. In this way, the image does not readily become a *continuing incarnation.* It does not readily become a link in the present between the worshipper and the object of his worship. Thus, the presence of statues or paintings or stained-glass windows in a church need not be violations of the second commandment. But when these images are used as links between the worshipper and God in prayer, except as a way to recall the memory of some mighty act of God, they become idols. [1]

5) I believe that pictures of Jesus may lawfully be used for illustrative purposes in Christian Education: in children's Bibles, in Sunday School curriculum, on flannel graphs, etc. Nothing in the Scriptures explicitly or implicitly forbids such educational aids.

6) This means primarily that historical scenes from Jesus' life may lawfully be depicted for artistic purposes

---

1. Gary North, *The Sinai Strategy* (Tyler, Texas: Institute for Christian Economics, 1986), 34.

in general culture as well. Artistic representations of Jesus humanity such as Rembrandt's *The Adoration of the Magi* and Caravaggio's *The Calling of St. Matthew* do not violate the second commandment.